W9-BIJ-491

OHIO

FAMILY ADVENTURE GUIDE™

by

KHRISTI SIGURDSON ZIMMETH

A VOYAGER BOOK

The Globe Pequot Press

OLD SAYBROOK, CONNECTICUT

Family Adventure Guide is a trademark of The Globe Pequot Press, Inc.

Cover and text design by Nancy Freeborn.

Library of Congress Cataloging-in-Publication Data

Zimmeth, Khristi Sigurdson.
    Family adventure guide: Ohio / by Khristi Sigurdson Zimmeth. — 1st ed.
       p.   cm. — (Family adventure guide series)
    "A voyager book."
    Includes index.
    ISBN 1-56440-864-7
    1. Ohio—Guidebooks. 2. Family recreation—Ohio—Guidebooks.
    I. Title. II. Series.
F489.3.Z57 1995
917.7104'43—dc20
                                                   95-39187
                                                    CIP

Manufactured in the United States of America
First Edition/Second Printing

To John, Nathaniel John, and Claire, who make coming home such a joy; and to my parents, who instilled in me a sense of wanderlust.

OHIO

Toledo

Cleveland

NORTHWEST

Mansfield

Akron

NORTHEAST

Bellefontaine

CENTRAL

Coshocton

Zoar
Steubenville

Piqua

Columbus

Dayton

Nelsonville

SOUTHWEST

Chillicothe

Marietta

Cincinnati

SOUTHEAST

Jackson

CONTENTS

ACKNOWLEDGMENTS

My thanks to all who contributed to the writing of this book, especially the incredibly organized folks at the Ohio Division of Travel and Tourism, and Mike Urban at Globe Pequot, who got the ball rolling.

INTRODUCTION

M y husband John and I took our son Nathaniel to Disney World when
he was nine weeks old. We were in Orlando for a few days, on an all-
too-brief break from a harsh Midwestern winter. We knew Nate
wouldn't get much out of the visit, but, kids at heart, we wanted to go.
And we made the most of it. We hammed it up with Mickey, sang
off-key with the Pirates of the Caribbean and took a trip around the world
at EPCOT Center while Nate slept peacefully in his carrier pack, oblivious
to the events, activities, and humanity swirling around him.

Now almost three, he's become a much more enthusiastic traveler.
With a travel writer for a Mom, he has to be.

Nate comes from a long line of wanderers. I grew up in a family that
believed in traveling together. By the time I was sixteen, our road trips had
taken in forty-eight of the fifty states (I've since made it to Alaska and as far
as Tahiti, but not yet to Hawaii) and filled countless scrapbooks and photo
albums.

One of our favorite states was Ohio, which we could get to in our
1969 Chevy Impala convertible from our home in Detroit without even a
bathroom break. In summer, we headed east along Lake Erie for the annual day at Cedar Point and south to Toledo for zoo treks or family reunions.
On longer trips we heated up with Skyline Chili in Cincinnati, cooled off
at Sea World near Cleveland, and braved the scream machines at King's
Island.

Years later, while working as an editor at *Travel & Leisure* magazine in New York, I covered Ohio as the magazine's midwestern editor. I assigned and wrote stories on the state's many attractions, from the largest Amish community in the world to the meandering tranquility of the Ohio River. I rediscovered along the way the beauty of America's seventeenth state.

Today, I once again hang my hat in the University of Michigan's Wolverine territory, but have strong ties to the Buckeye State. My sister-in-law lives in Columbus, a good friend lives in Cleveland, another has lived in Dayton and Cincinnati. From each, I received "inside information" on great places they discovered for their family and mine. Through the years, I've visited many of the places included in this book. (Ohio has hundreds of great places for families and I've tried to include as many of them as possible in this book. If I missed any that you'd like to see included in future editions, please write to me at The Globe Pequot Press, P.O. Box 833, Old Saybrook, CT 06475.)

What you hold in your hand is the sum of more than thirty years of exploring Ohio. I hope it inspires your family to plan trips of your own. Just remember to take a few bathroom breaks along the way.

— Khristi Sigurdson Zimmeth

The prices, rates, and other information listed in this guidebook were confirmed at press time. We recommend, however, that you call establishments to obtain current information before traveling.

NORTHWEST OHIO

Northwest Ohio is a patchwork quilt of many colors. It's home to historic small towns and big, industrial cities, as well as the gateway to the state's famed Lake Erie playground and some of the best walleye fishing in the world. You'll find attractions to suit nature lovers and nostalgia buffs, train aficionados and thrill seekers. And all throughout this corner of Ohio you'll find that special brand of friendliness that will be a hallmark of your travels and a long-lasting memory of your time in the Buckeye State.

TOLEDO

Toledo almost ended up as part of Michigan, its near northern neighbor. During the Toledo War of 1835–1836, it was claimed by both states. When the battle was over, the city was annexed to Ohio and the Northern Peninsula became part of Michigan.

It's not hard to see why it was in such demand. Today fun and friendly Toledo is a thriving industrial city and one of the world's busiest freshwater ports. **Promenade Park,** a peaceful, landscaped setting along the Maumee River, is still a favorite spot for watching the huge freighters and hardworking towboats that call the Great Lakes home. It's also the venue for weekend festivals, sailboat regattas, rowing competitions, powerboat races, and other colorful waterside entertainment.

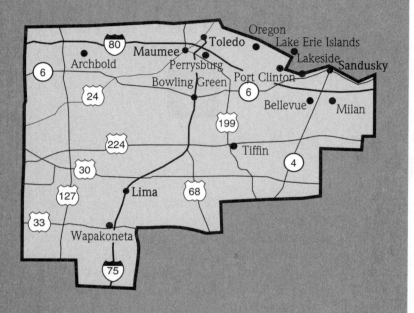

Oregon
Toledo
Maumee
Lake Erie Islands
Lakeside
Sandusky
Archbold
Perrysburg
Port Clinton
Bowling Green
Bellevue
Milan
Tiffin
Lima
Wapakoneta

80
6
24
6
199
224
30
4
127
68
33
75

Northwest Ohio

Freighter fans won't want to miss a visit to the *Willis B. Boyer,* docked at Toledo's International Park in the heart of downtown. The massive, 617-foot ship was launched in 1911 and retired in 1980. Today it depicts how the largest, most modern ship on the Great Lakes looked in its heyday and has been refurbished as a tribute to the city's rich port heritage and to the many freighters that continue to travel these waterways. For hours and information call (419) 698–8252.

Freighter watching make you hungry? Head across the river for a little sustenance, Toledo style. Your kids may have never heard of *M*A*S*H's* Corporal Klinger, but it won't matter once they're chowing on a chili sundae with a side of taco chips at **Tony Packo's Cafe.** Native son Jamie Farr, better known as the quirky, cross-dressing Corporal Klinger, grew up in this neighborhood bordering the river and brought this Hungarian-style eatery to national attention when he starred on the long-running hit series in the 1970s and 1980s. Farr raved about the eatery during seven different episodes of *M*A*S*H* and still visits a few times a year to get his fill of Packo's chili dogs.

The cafe had been a local favorite for decades before it was "discovered" by the *M*A*S*H* audiences. Tony Packo, Sr., opened the unassuming storefront restaurant, then just a bar and a few tables, in 1933, with a few old Hungarian family recipes. It soon caught on, and the cafe expanded into adjacent buildings as business grew.

Tony, Jr., has added family entertainment, including magicians on weekends and a children's menu, with classics such as peanut butter and jelly, grilled cheese, and American-style hot dogs. Despite recent additions, visitors of all ages still opt for the house specialties: stuffed cabbage, with almost a pound of meat wrapped in a cabbage leaf and smothered with tomato sauce; tangy chicken paprikash; or the signature chili dog, with sausage and Packo's famous chili.

That chili dog and its fans are memorialized throughout the restaurant. Legend has it that Packo's wife started the tradition when Burt Reynolds visited in 1973. Seeking something more original for his autograph, she had him sign a hot dog bun. Today, Reynolds's signature is just one of hundreds on the walls from celebrities that range from musician Frank Zappa ("Great Buns") to Roseanne Barr, Steve Martin, Bill Cosby,

Kevin Costner, even Margaret Thatcher, and President Clinton. Tony Packo's Cafe is at 1902 Front Street, call (419) 691–6054 for more information. On the same side of the river, a little farther west, is the **U.S. Glass Specialty Outlet.** The Libbey corporation was founded here, and glass figures prominently in the city's history and psyche. Although Libbey no longer gives factory tours, glassblowing and manufacturing can still be seen at the outlet, part of the Custom Deco Corporation, makers of ceramic and glass wares. Their high-quality goods are sold nationally through department stores such as Jacobson's and Elder Beerman.

Glassblowers are on duty every day except Monday from 11:00 A.M. to 4:00 P.M. Excitement heats up along with the glass as they fashion molten material into items ranging from paperweights to vases. Three rooms are open to the public; everything (of course) is for sale as well, some at discounted prices. The outlet is at 1367 Miami Street, call (419) 698–8046 for information.

Glass figures prominently over at the **Toledo Museum of Art** as well. Museums can be stuffy and lifeless—or they can be like this lively arts institution. Visit on a Saturday and you're likely to encounter young aficionados everywhere—lounging outside near larger-than-life abstract sculpture such as Mel Kendrick's *Sculpture No. 4,* sketching in the galleries, or taking a class or workshop at the adjacent art school.

Local residents are justifiably proud of this small but choice museum. All the big names are here: El Greco, Rubens, Van Gogh, Picasso, Monet, Matisse—and more. Founded in 1901 with funds from the Libbey Glass family, its collection today spans 5,000 years and almost as many cultures. Not surprisingly, the museum has one of the best collections of art in glass found anywhere in the world. Airy and light-filled, it's a pleasure to explore.

A good way to get acquainted is to catch the 4½-minute video shown continuously in the lobby. After that, head past the large, colorful Matisse cutout of Apollo, made from radiant shards of blues, oranges, and reds, and take the stairs to the second floor, where you'll find the majority of the permanent galleries.

Indiana Jones wannabes won't want to miss the Egyptian room, where a well-preserved mummy from the ancient city of Akmin dates from

KHRISTI'S TOP FAMILY ADVENTURES IN NORTHWEST OHIO

1. Cedar Point, Sandusky
2. Maumee Bay State Park, Oregon
3. Lake Erie Islands
4. Toledo Zoo, Toledo
5. Neil Armstrong Air and Space Museum, Wapakoneta

the 304–30 B.C. Ptolemaic period and fascinates amateur archaeologists of all ages. Would-be warriors can press a button in the African gallery and listen to a wooden slit drum, circa 1900–1925, pound out messages or imagine what it would be like to wear one of the heavy and intricately beaded headdresses from Zaire. Is surrealism more your style? Challenge your kids to see how many different tools they can find incorporated into Jim Dine's *The Crommelynck Gate* (1983).

One of the best things about visiting a museum is discovering how people lived in other times. Portraits of children—from Dutch painter Carel Fabritius's *The Happy Child* from 1645 to Abbott Handerson Thayer's *Portrait of Helen Sears* from 1891–1892—provide grounds for studying both similarities and differences. The museum is at 2445 Monroe Street, admission is free. Hours are 10:00 A.M. to 4:00 P.M. Tuesday through Saturday; 1:00 to 5:00 P.M. on Sunday. For more information call (419) 255–8000.

The residential area surrounding the museum is known as Toledo's **Historic Old West End.** Bounded by Monroe, Collingwood, and Detroit, the area encompasses twenty-five city blocks, making it one of the largest collections of late Victorian houses in the United States. Fine examples of stately Colonial, Georgian, Italianate, Queen Anne, and other designs line the sidewalks, all meticulously restored by the proud owners. A walking-tour brochure is available by calling (419) 259-5207.

Back downtown, head for the latest addition to Toledo's waterfront—the **Center of Science and Industry,** better known as COSI. Be the first on your block to visit the outpost of the popular science museum headquartered in Columbus when it opens late in 1996. This hands-on, interactive museum—one of the biggest things to hit Toledo in years—will focus on the wonders of the world of science and include a number of special displays that trace the city's history, including glassmaking and automotive exhibits. Call (419) 249-5242 for more information and opening dates.

A favorite spot for viewing the wonders of the natural world is the **Toledo Zoo,** located a few miles from downtown. This respected zoo, founded in 1899, houses more than 3,000 animals representing 525 species on fifty-one acres. Clever BETCHA DIDN'T KNOW signs posted throughout give unusual facts and figures about zoo inhabitants.

Ever come nose to nose with a hippo? You will at the world's only "Hippoquarium," voted one of the ten best animal exhibits in the country by *USA Today Weekend.* Two Nile hippos appear almost graceful as they dog-paddle around an underwater viewing area. Visitors have witnessed three live underwater births since the attraction opened in 1986. The 8-foot-deep pool holds 360 gallons of water that are pumped through four, 8,000-gallon filters every 90 minutes.

Go on safari in the African Savannah, where you can explore the naturally landscaped environment while searching for lions, giraffes, rhinos, meerkats (they look something like a gopher), and other animals that roam freely. Watch the pandas wash themselves like cats. Marvel at the tree-climbing koalas—the Toledo Zoo is one of only twelve zoos in the United States to permanently exhibit these cuddly animals.

The zoo takes its educational mission seriously—but not at the expense of fun. Your kids won't care that the Diversity of Life exhibit won a Significant Achievement Award from the American Zoological Association, but they won't be able to keep their hands off the exhibit's microscopes and magnifying glasses that allow them to examine the delicate wings of a tiny blue butterfly or watch tarantulas crawling around their well-fortified box.

Other family favorites: the reptile building, where a huge Burmese python holds court among other lesser reptiles; the friendlier species in the Children's Zoo, including Tony the llama, Buckie the horse, and Nugget, the Vietnamese potbellied pig; and the extensive Kingdom of the Apes, new in 1993, where you can watch the antics of orangutans, chimps, and gorillas.

If the animal kingdom loses its appeal, head for the old-fashioned carousel, the playground (where kids can pretend to be a butterfly, a spider, or a warthog), or rest weary feet with a ride on the tiny red train that circles the zoo grounds. Or head for the **Elephant's Trunk Gift Shop,** where you can stock up on souvenirs of your visit, with wares from T-shirts and rubber animals to penguin-shaped sidewalk chalk and even Zoo Doo, organic compost made from animal droppings.

Don't leave without having a bite in the recently renovated **Carnivore Cafe.** Dedicated in 1927 as the Carnivora Building, it was once home to the zoo's primates and large cats. Now you're the species behind bars as you nosh on hamburgers, hot dogs, and other deli-style snacks in the same cages that once housed the zoo's largest animals. The zoo also has a respected greenhouse and well-tended gardens. The zoo is 4 miles south of downtown Toledo and is open year-round except holidays. Hours are 10:00 A.M. to 6:00 P.M. daily. Admission is $5.00 for adults; $2.50 for children. For more information call (419) 385–5721.

More beautiful blooms can be found at the **Toledo Botanical Gardens,** considered by many to be among the best in the state. This picturesque sixty-two-acre setting of meadows and gardens boasts fragrant herbs, roses, and colorful wildflowers. Browse in artists' galleries, or peruse the many tempting offerings in the gardens' gift shop. Special events for families include the cafe concerts and the popular Ghosts In The Garden program. The gardens are open year-round from dawn to dusk. For more information call (419) 936–2986.

The **Stranaham Arboretum**, part of the University of Toledo, also has gorgeous grounds to stroll and more than forty-seven beautiful acres that entice growing green thumbs. Among the highlights are more than two thousand woody plants representing 450 varieties, fifty-four maple species, and forty-eight varieties of fragrant, flowering crab. It's a great place to introduce your kids to the natural world. The arboretum is at 4131 Pantera Drive. For information, call (419) 882–6806.

MAUMEE

If you've ever sat through nine endless innings of major-league baseball and wondered what happened to the kind of game you remember from your childhood, look no further then the **Toledo Mud Hens,** who play in nearby suburban Maumee. The stars may argue about contracts and endorsements, but back in the minor leagues, you'll still hear old-fashioned cries of "Play Ball."

This is the life chronicled in the hit movie *Bull Durham.* The stadiums are smaller, and fans can get box seats for just a few bucks. At Toledo's **Ned Skeldon Stadium**—part of the Lucas County Fairgrounds in Maumee—the best seats in the house sell for a cool $5.00 each.

The Mud Hens are a Detroit Tigers farm team. Part of the International League, they step up to the plate against rivals such as the Charlotte Knights (affiliated with the Florida Marlins), the Columbus Clippers (New York Yankees), the Pawtucket Red Sox (Boston Red Sox), and the Richmond Braves (Atlanta Braves).

Besides all the regularly scheduled fun, there are special events such as Disco Night, Martian Antenna Night, Friendly's Muddy's Birthday Bash (in honor of Muddy, the Mud Hens' mascot), and Fright Night. There's also the annual Detroit Tigers/Toledo Tussle, complete with a baseball card show, held each July. The Mud Hens are at 2901 Key Street in Maumee. For tickets call (419) 893–9483.

Old-fashioned fun of a different kind can be had at the **Wolcott House Museum Complex** on River Road. The restored buildings, including a furnished Federal-style house circa 1836, a log cabin, train depot, farmhouse, and 1840s Greek Revival style home, offer a picture of what family life was like in the Maumee Valley in the years leading up to the Civil War. The complex is open 1:00 to 4:00 P.M. Wednesday through Sunday, April through December. For more information call (419) 893–9602.

ARCHBOLD

Homage to the past is also paid at the **Sauder Farm and Craft Village** off State Road 2 in nearby Archbold. Explore what life in mid-1800s rural Ohio was like by watching blacksmiths, potters, and glassblowers practice their arts at this fascinating living-history complex dedicated to fine all-American craftsmanship. With more than thirty buildings clustered around a central axis, you can easily spend a full day exploring here.

The pace is slow and the staff friendly. Don't miss the huge quilt shop, general store (with lots of old-fashioned penny candy for little sweet tooths) or the simple but delicious lunches offered year-round at the country-style **Barn Restaurant** (yes, it was a real barn). Popular weekend events in season include fiddlers' contests, a doll show and sale in August, apple butter making in September, and a whittlin' and woodcarvin' show in October. Tickets are $8.00 for adults; $4.00 for students; free for children age five and under. There's also a handy thirty-seven-site adjacent campground. The village is open daily from late April to October. For more information call (800) 590–9755.

PERRYSBURG

The land south of Toledo is also home to reconstructed **Fort Meigs,** the largest wooden-walled fortification in America. The sound of fife and drums and the smell of gunpowder transports visitors of all ages back to the time of the War of 1812, when the fort was built. Constructed by General William Henry Harrison (later President Harrison) in 1813, it defended the area then known as Ohio Country against two sieges by the British and was used as a staging point for the retaking of Detroit and the invasion of Canada.

The reconstruction, begun in 1865, recreates the stockade as it looked during the first British siege of 1813. The fort's seven blockhouses appear as they did then, with 2-feet thick walls, 4-inch-deep window and cannon-port shutters, and whitewashed interior walls. Several buildings contain fascinating exhibits and dioramas on the War of 1812, the fort's reconstruction, and the lives of the soldiers who were garrisoned here during the war.

Kids can view a six-pound cannon and the implements used to fire it, and peer out of second-floor gun ports, where soldiers took aim at a foreign enemy. On the Grand Battery, you can stand where General Harrison did when he watched as members of the Kentucky militia were trapped and taken prisoner on the other side of the Maumee River. On the Grand Parade, you can almost hear the barking of the sergeant as you imagine soldiers receiving orders for the day, obtaining their whiskey rations, or going about their daily work.

Cannon demonstrations are held hourly and are a favorite of young military fans. Special events include reenactments, military encampments, and summer commemorative weekends. Open Wednesday through Sunday during the summer, weekends the rest of the year, the fort is at 2900 West River Road, call (419) 874–4121.

OREGON

Had enough history for awhile? When you're ready for some sun and surf (or, depending on the season, some snow and cross-country skiing) follow the sandy shores of Lake Erie to **Maumee Bay State Park.** Ohio is well known for its seventy-two excellent state parks, and this one is considered among the best.

Families tired of the at-best rustic cabins found in many parks will be pleasantly surprised by the modern "lodge" that looks more like an expensive, state-of-the-art hotel. It was added in 1991. Accommodations include 120 guest rooms in the main hotel and twenty two- or four-bedroom furnished cottages (reserve well in advance), with screened-in porches and fireplaces set in the park's wetlands.

And if birdwatching, bicycling, and sunsets over Lake Erie aren't enough to fill a visit, there's also an indoor and outdoor pool, beach, tennis, racquetball and basketball courts, restaurants and lounges, an exercise room and sauna, a nature center, playground, and an eighteen-hole Scottish-style golf course and amphitheater. Rates vary by room size and season. The park is at 1750 Park Road, #2; call (419) 836–1466 for reservations and other information.

Not surprisingly, **Lake Erie fishing** is a popular sport at the Maumee Bay State Park and in other parts of Northwest Ohio. Your amateur anglers will fall hook, line, and sinker for the tasty but testy walleye, who bite here from mid-May through mid-October. They're so numerous that Lake Erie's western basin is known as the Walleye Capital Of The World, providing nearly two-thirds of the fish harvested from Ohio's Lake Erie waters each year. While walleye and yellow perch are among the most popular catches for Lake Erie fishermen, other common species include white bass, smallmouth bass, freshwater drum, channel catfish, and white perch. For the truly hearty, ice fishing is popular on the lake during the months of January and February. Just be sure to remember the long underwear. For more information on Erie County fishing call (800) 255–ERIE.

PORT CLINTON

Follow along the western shores of Lake Erie, and you'll soon reach **African Wildlife Safari Park.** Don your safari hats, but forget those scenes from *Jurassic Park*—the most dangerous thing you're likely to encounter is lovable llamas, amiable alpacas, and friendly zebras, all of which wander aimlessly around your family car or van as you drive through the 100-acre enclave, the only drive-through safari park in the Midwest. A bucket of food is included in the admission price, and the more aggressive animals come up to beg, leaving long, wet tongue marks on the side of your car or van.

The park, open seasonally, boasts one of the largest alpaca and llama exhibits in the United States, as well as two rare white zebras, two of only a few in the world and the only ones in the United States. More than 400 animals roam free among the park's grasslands.

Longing to get a little closer? Take a free ride on a pony or a camel, pet an ostrich, or feed the baby animals in **Safari Junction.** Burn off a little energy in the new **Jungle Junction Playland,** or fuel up at the Mobassa Cafe or one of the many picnic areas in Safari Junction. Afterward, check out the popular "Porkchop Downs" pig races and other types of amusing animal entertainment held daily during the summer.

Don't leave without casting a vote in the park's "Beauty or Beast" contest. A special exhibit featuring the rare African warthog (officially known as the tongue-twisting *Phacochoerus aethiopicus* but nicknamed "Buford") asks you to rate the looks of the warthog. The park calls him the world's ugliest animal, but others find his quirky looks appealing. You decide. The park, open May through September, is at 267 Lightner Road. Admission is $10.95 per adult, $6.95 per child. For more information contact (419) 732-3606.

LAKE ERIE ISLANDS

It doesn't take long to reach the Lake Erie Islands—just a short ferryboat ride from Port Clinton or Sandusky—but you'll swear you've traveled much farther. There's an otherworldly feeling about this string of islands 12 miles from Sandusky. The movie *Somewhere In Time* may have been filmed on Michigan's Mackinac Island, but it could easily have taken place here. A number of companies offer frequent ferry runs (hourly in summer) that transport you back and forth easily from the mainland to three of the five islands.

Each has its own appeal. **Kelley's Island** is the most remote and offers a great escape for the adventurous family or one seeking an easy going vacation unspoiled by other people or cars. The largest American island on Lake Erie, the entire island is listed in the National Register of Historic Places.

Once on the island, most visitors get to the pristine shoreline and the island's two popular archaeological sites by biking or driving golf carts (rentals are available).

Glacial Grooves State Memorial on the island's north side features smooth black limestone gullies carved some 30,000 years ago by Ice Age glaciers. This 400-foot-long stretch is considered one of the finest glacial markings in the United States. Kelley's Island also boasts the fine **Inscription Rock State Memorial,** found on the south side. Prehistoric pictographs show various animal forms and human figures smoking pipes and wearing headdresses. They were carved by Native Americans from the Erie tribe, who were attracted here by the abundant fish in the area (walleye and perch are still island specialties; they can be had with hand-dipped onion rings at the popular **Village Pump** restaurant in the small village).

Hiking fans? Acres of uninterrupted countryside, mostly preserved through state ownership, provide miles of trails. Lace up and head for the

TOP ANNUAL EVENTS IN NORTHWEST OHIO

Crosby Festival of the Arts, June, Toledo; (419) 535–9101
Lucas County Fair, July, Maumee; (419) 321–6404
Festival of Flight, July, Wapakoneta; (419) 738–8811
Allen County Fair, August, Lima; (419) 228–7141
Melon Festival, September, Milan; (419) 499–2766

wooded **North Shore Loop Trail.** Cedar trees and milkweed, covered with Monarch butterflies, blanket the East Quarry Trail, where even pint-sized geologists will unearth fossils and other natural treasures. For more information on the island and its offerings contact the Chamber of Commerce at (419) 746–2360.

If you and your kids like a little more man-made excitement, consider a stay at **Put-in-Bay,** the bustling port on **South Bass Island.** You'll find wildlife of another kind on this island, which was named for its sheltered harbor that protected sailors during stormy weather. It's been sheltering families looking for sun and fun ever since.

Here you can climb the steps and take in the great view 352 feet above the **Perry's Victory and Peace Monument** (there's also an elevator for the unadventurous). The monument was named for Commodore Oliver Perry, who sought refuge on the island during the War of 1812. Its observation deck offers breathtaking views of the neighboring islands and Lake Erie's blue expanse.

Perry is also the namesake and the 1813 discoverer of **Perry's Cave** (419–285–2405), which takes spelunkers on twenty-minute tours more than 50 feet below the surface of South Bass Island. Tradition has it that Perry stored supplies and kept prisoners in the cave during the battle of Lake Erie.

Just a half-mile from downtown, the cave is 208 feet long by 165 feet wide. It was first shown to the public in 1870 for the grand fee of 10 cents per person (today it's slightly more). The walls, ceiling, and cave floor are covered with calcium carbonate that settled from centuries of dripping water; an underground lake, where the water level rises and falls with Lake Erie, is located inside as well. At one time the island's Victory Hotel, once the largest in the world, pumped its water from the cave's lake. Today, visitors can still see the ruins of that hotel, which burned in 1919 in South Bass Island State Park. The cave also offers spooky lantern tours, a shaded picnic area, and a "Shop On The Top," where kids can mine for gems or pick up a memento of their adventure. The cave is open daily throughout the summer from 11:00 A.M. to 6:00 P.M.

Put-in-Bay is also home to **Crystal Cave** (419–285–2811), which workers found in 1897 when digging a well on the island. Exploration found the 40-foot pocket they had dug to be part of a geode (hollow pockets that are lined with beautiful sparkling crystals). Today, Crystal Cave is known as the world's largest geode. Samples of the largest celestite crystals found here are now part of the exhibition at the Smithsonian Institution in Washington, D.C. Put-in-Bay is accessible from Port Clinton and Catawba Point, west of Sandusky.

The fishing on **Middle Bass Island** has been attracting anglers— including Presidents Harrison and Cleveland—for years. Once called Isle de Fleurs, or flower island, by missionaries who visited in 1680, Middle Bass and its neighbors North and Small Bass are named, not surprisingly, for the abundant smallmouth bass swimming in these waters.

Middle Bass is a serene island of great natural beauty. The historic **Lonz Winery**, established in 1864 as the Golden Eagle Wine Company, offers tours of its century-old cellars, dug by hand during the Civil War, and its castlelike architecture. Tours include a multimedia presentation, cellar tours, and a tasting. Although wine is no longer produced on the island, Lonz maintains Concord and Catawba vineyards here and sends the harvest to the mainland for processing. The winery is open May through September. For information call (419) 285–5411. For camping and fishing information on Middle Bass call (419) 285–6121.

LAKESIDE

Looking for a little peace and quiet on your next vacation? Back on the mainland, look no further than **Lakeside,** the idyllic community known as the "Chautauqua On Lake Erie." Families have been coming to this historic Victorian community on the Marblehead Peninsula, east of Port Clinton, since the turn of the century.

Religious leaders once gathered here for spiritual retreat and rebirth. As more and more families joined them, Lakeside became increasingly known as a family vacation paradise. Today, although religious life is still an important part of the Lakeside season, the emphasis is on fellowship, personal growth, and arts appreciation.

Day-visitors can pick up a daily pass that entitles them to enjoy activities that range from the Lakeside Symphony, ballet companies, lectures, and choral events to free-wheeling children's programs. At any given time during the summer season, the grounds and the huge 700-foot dock are alive with families swimming, sailing, fishing, strolling, or simply enjoying another beautiful day on the water.

Hoping to spend the night? Lodging is available at the grand 100-room, Victorian-style **Hotel Lakeside** (with its great view of Lake Erie from the huge porch), at the more modern **Fountain Inn,** as well as at bed and breakfasts throughout the area. Cottages are also available for rent. For more information on Lakeside contact the association at (419) 798–4461.

MARBLEHEAD

Not far from Lakeside, lighthouse enthusiasts of all ages make a beeline for the oldest operating lighthouse on the Great Lakes. The **Marblehead Lighthouse** is also one of the most scenic and a great spot for a family photo. Built in 1821, this 85-foot-tall limestone light was constructed in just eleven weeks. The first keeper, Benajah Wolcott, kept the thirteen lamps fueled by whale oil; later the whale oil was replaced by a Fresnel lens, imported from France in 1903. Updated with electricity in 1923, the lighthouse retired its lens in 1969. Today, the lighthouse's new 300mm light flashes a green glow every three seconds. Tours are offered one

Saturday per month from June through September. For information call the Peninsula Chamber of Commerce, P.O. Box 268, Marblehead, (419) 798–9777.

The area around the lighthouse is also home to a small artists' community located at the peninsula's tip and to the busiest U.S. Coast Guard station on the Great Lakes. Only a few hundred yards down Bayshore Road, a historic marker identifies the causeway leading to **Johnson's Island,** with its famous Civil War Confederate Prison Camp.

Originally named Bull's Island (prisoners referred to the prison as the Bull Pen), the island's 330 acres on Sandusky Bay were home to some 9,000 Confederate officers, Union defectors, and civilians between 1862 and 1865. Of the original 9,000, some 206 remain on the island, memorialized in white marble in the island's cemetery. It's a fascinating—if sobering—piece of Ohio history.

SANDUSKY

When I was a kid, summer began the day my family went to **Cedar Point.** My sister and I looked forward to it each year. As school drew to a close, we'd start badgering our parents about our annual trek to the amusement park, and we didn't let up till we were in the car and heading east.

Almost thirty years later, Cedar Point remains one of Ohio's top family destinations. And much of what draws them is what drew us all those years ago—roller coasters (the most in the world), snow cones, sun, and fun.

Now in its 125th year, Cedar Point has changed since the days when its biggest attraction was a dance hall. Today it is best known for its eleven scream machines (including the 205-foot-tall Magnum XL-200, the soaring Raptor, the Mean Streak, and the wicked thirteen-story Demon Drop) and fifty-six more down-to-earth rides spread out over 364 acres.

But there are options to being spun, twisted, dropped or turned upside-down. Check out the IMAX film at the Cinema. Come nose to nose with performing sea creatures at the Oceana Stadium. Wander the Lake Erie beach and boardwalk. Dance along to live stage shows. Get away from it all on the cable cars or space spiral.

Little ones have their own pint-size fun, with seventeen miniature rides in Kiddy Kingdom, including a small-scale roller coaster, bumper boats, and a drive-it-yourself four-by-four truck that looks just like the grown-up model. There's barnyard fun at the petting farm and the popular Berenstain Bear Country, with tree houses, ball crawls, and other playground favorites.

And if all that wasn't enough, there's Challenge Park and the new-and-improved Soak City Water Park, which recently doubled in size, with three new rides, including a gigantic, high-action water slide, featuring six-person rafts, an inner-tube river adventure, and two new playground areas (both parks are separate admissions).

Looking for a great place to stay? The historic 1905 **Hotel Breakers** underwent a $10 million facelift in 1995, adding 206 new units to this resort that has housed luminaries such as Abbott and Costello, Annie Oakley, and six U.S. Presidents.

Water-loving thrill seekers won't want to miss this high-action water slide at Cedar Point's Soak City Water Park. (Courtesy Cedar Point)

Admission is $26.95 for ages four through fifty-nine, 48 inches and taller; $4.95 for ages four and older, under 48 inches; $15.95 for age 60 and older. For more information call (419) 627–2350.

Merry-go-rounds may seem a trifle tame after a day at Cedar Point, but they have a certain nostalgic charm that's perennially appealing—especially to toddlers and younger children who may be a little overwhelmed by Cedar Point's frantic pace. Relive the glory days of the carousel and other classic Americana with a tour of the five-year-old **Merry-Go-Round Museum,** housed in the city's former 1920s downtown post office.

Highlights include the working Allen Herschell carousel from the 1930s (a free ride is given as part of the tour) and the original Gustav Dentzel carving shop from Philadelphia. There's also a small English carousel from the turn of the century, a gift shop stocking virtually every carousel-related item known to man, traveling exhibitions, and a full-time, on-premises carver/restorer. Open year-round, admission is $4.00 for adults; $3.00 for children aged four through fourteen; free for kids under age three. For more information contact the Merry-Go-Round Museum, P.O. Box 718, Sandusky, or call (419) 626–6111.

Sandusky is also home to a number of companies that offer day cruises in and around the Lake Erie islands. For the first-time visitor, this is the perfect way to get a handle on what the area holds and where you'd like to come back to next time. Many cruise companies offer meals as part of the package.

The *Emerald Empress,* part of the Neuman Cruise and Ferry Line, is a 150-foot, three-deck cruise boat that accommodates up to 600 people on twelve different cruises. Lazy Day Cruises head for Put-in-Bay and Kelley's Island, with continental breakfast and lunch en route. Lunchbreak and Dinner Cruises include an hour-and-a-half sightseeing cruise around the islands and Sandusky Bay, and feature an on-board buffet. Saturday Prime-Time Cruises include a hand-carved prime rib dinner and a dance band. Sunday-Brunch Cruises and Lakebreak sightseeing cruises are also offered. Prices range from $5.25 to $29.95 per person. For more information call (800) 876–1907 or (419) 626–5557.

Two other companies offer popular island cruises. The *M.V. City of Sandusky,* docked at the foot of Columbus Avenue in downtown

Sandusky, is a 300-passenger boat with full-bar service, dance floor, sundeck and snack bar. Daily tours include visits to Kelley's Island, Put-in-Bay, and Lonz Winery on Middle Bass Island. Tickets are $22.50 per person for adults; $12.00 for children age four to eleven. For more information call (800) 426–6286 or (419) 627–0198.

Looking for a good time? Look no further than the *Goodtime I,* docked at Jackson Street Pier, which offers daily tours to Kelley's Island and Put-in-Bay. The *Goodtime I* is a 365-passenger boat with full-bar service, dance floor, and snack bar. Rates are $19.95 for adults; $9.95 for children age four to twelve. Call (800) 446–3140.

After a relaxing cruise, be sure to stop to get in a lick or two at **Toft's Dairy** near the edge of town. This local dairy has been serving up creamy confections since 1900, when they were founded as a small farm with a respected herd of dairy cattle. In 1935 they acquired another retail dairy, the beginnings of the modern operation. Today they've moved three times, service towns as far as Michigan and outlying parts of Ohio, and are the only locally owned and operated dairy on Lake Erie between Lorain and Toledo.

Tours are offered daily. Afterward, sample classic flavors such as butter pecan and vanilla or the newer favorites, such as Moose Tracks and Mother Lode, full of chocolate and caramel. Kids often opt for the chewy Dinosaur Crunch. Toft's is at 3717 Venice Road, on the city's outskirts; call (419) 625–4376.

Sandusky is also home to **Lagoon Deer Park,** off Route 269. Here you can get up close and personal with more than 250 animals from Europe, Japan, Asia, South and North America, and more. Hand-feed hundreds of deer and other tame species, feed fish, or cast your pole in stocked lagoons and fishing lakes. If you visit in the spring, look for the park's newest additions—seventy-five baby animals are born here each year. Don't miss the famous "Dancing Chicken." The grounds also have attractive picnic facilities; open mid-April through mid-October. For hours and more information call (419) 684–5701.

MILAN

About 13 miles south of Sandusky is **Thomas Edison's Birthplace.** This simple seven-room, 2½-story home built in 1841 housed the famous inventor of the phonograph and the lightbulb from the time he was born in 1847 until he was seven years old, when the family moved to Port Huron, Michigan. The museum was opened by his daughter on February 11, 1947—the day he would have turned 100.

Today it's still run by his great-grandson and furnished with many original family pieces. Don't miss the room honoring his many inventions, including phonographs, lightbulbs, and models of his movie studio and Menlo Park laboratory. Other examples of Edisonia include examples of his early inventions, documents, and family mementos.

The adjacent **Milan Historical Museum** has old-fashioned dolls and glassware, a blacksmith's shop, and a vintage general store. The museum is closed in December and January. For information on the birthplace call (419) 499–2135; for the museum, (419) 499–2968.

BELLEVUE

Southeast of Milan is Bellevue, where you can "go underground" during a visit to **Seneca Caverns,** located south of Bellevue on State Road 269. This 110-foot-deep cave—technically an earth crack—was discovered in 1872 by two boys hunting rabbits, when their dog fell into what they thought was a sinkhole.

The cavern opened to the public in 1933. Today, visitors descend steps 110 feet underground through seven levels to an underground river on hour-long tours that are offered from May 1 through October 15. The largest room is 250 feet in length. The cavern is fairly rugged—a fact kids love—and is one of the few in the country kept in its original natural condition. Don't leave without panning for gems at the Sandy Creek Gem Mining or enjoying a picnic in the shade. The cavern is open Memorial Day through Labor Day and weekends in May, September, and through mid-October. For more information call (419) 483–6711.

Bellevue is also home to historic **Lyme Village,** a tribute to a local farmer named John Wright, who did well and went on to build an impressive Victorian mansion, complete with a third-floor ballroom. Today that mansion is joined by fifteen other buildings to create a re-creation of an Ohio village, Victorian-style. Besides the residence there are three log houses, a schoolhouse, a farm, general store, hardware store, post office, and more. Daily demonstrations of spinning, weaving, blacksmithing, and candlemaking offer children a fascinating glimpse of a bygone American way of life. For more information call (419) 483–4949.

TIFFIN

"Wanna try a hot one?" an operator asks as he holds out a tray of sizzling potato chips to a young visitor who, not surprisingly, answers in the affirmative. Some 2,000 pounds of chips roll off the assembly line each day, more than 40 million pounds each year, at **Ballreich's** before they end up in grocery stores throughout Ohio and as part of family picnics across the state.

The company was founded in the 1920s by Fred and Ethel Ballreich, who once started each day peeling the potatoes for their chips by hand, later delivering them in brown paper bags secured with staples to local retailers. These days it's a much more sophisticated process. Today it takes only eighteen minutes to go from raw potato to crispy bagged chips.

Hundreds of chip lovers take the thirty-minute free tour in which they watch the peeling, cutting, and frying process, and learn how spuds are transformed into tasty snacks. Tours are offered on Monday, Tuesday, Thursday, and Friday every half hour from 8:00 A.M. to 9:30 A.M. Along the way, you'll learn about Ballreich's process and even some chip-lovers' trivia, including the fact that potato chips were first introduced in Saratoga Springs, New York, as a practical joke and that brown chips are naturally higher in sugar and not burnt. There's an added bonus: Visitors receive a free sample bag at the end of the tour; they can also pick up a bag of the popular flavors such as Regular, Barbecue, Sour Cream and Onion, Southwest Barbecue, Salt and Vinegar and even Salt-Free in the retail store on the premises. Ballreich's is at 186 Ohio Avenue; for tour times call (419) 447–1814.

Potato chips aren't the only product for which the area is known. **Maxwell Crystal,** on Madison Street, also gives tours. Wander through the company's production facilities on one of three free guided tours, and you'll watch Maxwell's signature glassblowing and glass-engraving employees at work. There's a gift shop on the premises; for information call (419) 448–4286.

Show your kids the finished product at the **Seneca County Museum,** 28 Clay Street, which displays a rare and extensive grouping of Tiffin glass, including early Victorian pieces in a well-preserved historic house (circa 1853). For information, call (419) 447–5955. Last but not least, the **Glass Heritage Gallery,** about 14 miles away in nearby Fostoria, houses a fine collection of glass made in Fostoria plants from 1887 to 1920. Examples include lamps, crystal bowls, art glass, and more. Hours vary; call (419) 435–5077.

While Northwest Ohio is known far and wide for its lakeshore, the southern part of the region offers many family attractions as well. Zip south along Interstate 75 and you'll pass a number of spots well worth a stop.

BOWLING GREEN

You can't miss Bowling Green. The signs for Bowling Green State University are the first clue that you're getting close, followed by the huge football stadium. The university dominates the town and is known for its attractive, 1,300-acre campus surrounded by fertile farmland.

So it's not surprising to find the **Educational Memorabilia Center** here. This one-room schoolhouse from 1875 was moved from Norwalk, Ohio, 60 miles to the east, and rebuilt in 1975 in time for the country's bicentennial.

After a visit, your kids may never gripe about going to school again. The schoolhouse is decorated with furnishings typical of the era—potbellied stove, fabric blackboard, uncomfortable wooden desks. Two doors mark the entrance—one for boys, one for girls. Display cases house memorabilia such as the center's collection of rare McGuffey reading charts, a century-old ketchup bottle that was found when the building was dismantled, and even a tombstone that formed the original school sign (tour guides speculate that it was an early attempt at recycling). On-premises tour guides give twenty-minute lectures about school life at the time. Hours are limited, and the center is closed when the university is not in session. For more information call (419) 372–7405.

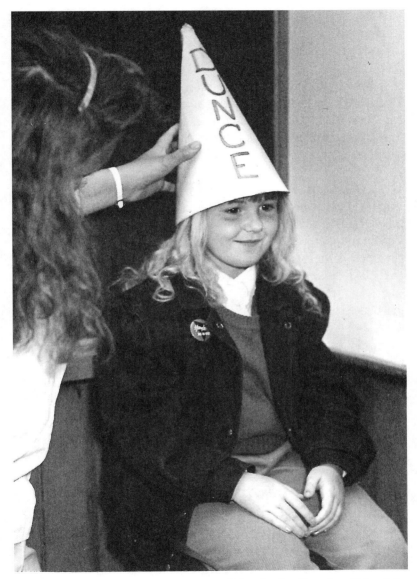

Children can learn what school was like in the 1800s at Bowling Green State University's Little Red Schoolhouse, which is part of the Educational Memorabilia Center. (Courtesy the Educational Memorabilia Center)

Bowling Green is also home to the **National Tractor Pulling Championship,** the world's largest outdoor tractor pull, held each year in late August at the Wood County Fairgrounds. For information, call (419) 354–1434.

If you visit in winter, make snowshoe tracks to the **Mary Jane Thurston State Park,** not far away, near Napoleon. This 555-acre park has fishing, boating, and hiking in summer but is renowned in the area for its exciting downhill sledding. For more information call (419) 832–7662.

LIMA

Venture a little farther south along I–75 and you'll hit Lima. This small city, nicknamed "Ohio's Hometown" is also home to the **U.S. Plastics Corporation,** one of the area's largest employers. Visitors can get an up-close view of the rotational mold process used in producing industrial plastic containers during a guided walking tour and then take advantage of discounts on more than 13,000 home, office, and garden plastic products in the outlet store. U.S. Plastics is at 1390 Neubrecht Road; call (419) 228–2242.

After the tour, stop for lunch at the **Old Barn Out Back Restaurant,** a local family-style favorite. Try the lunch buffet (choose from old-fashioned baked ham, fried chicken, or country roast beef) and go back for seconds (or thirds) at the all-you-can-eat soup/salad/bread/dessert bar. Take along a few of their famous cinnamon rolls topped with cinnamon butter for the road, or better yet, go back for breakfast. The restaurant is at 3135 West Elm Street; call (419) 991–3075.

WAPAKONETA

Wapakoneta has one main claim to fame: It put the first man on the moon. On July 20, 1969, one tiny step for Neil Armstrong became a giant leap for mankind when he forever changed the face of American space exploration. Enthusiasts and sci-fi buffs won't want to miss the white-domed **Neil Armstrong Air and Space Museum,** which honors Armstrong and others who have contributed to man's exploration of space and sky.

I–75 drivers can't help but notice the museum's stark white dome from the freeway. The museum opened in 1972 and reflects the boldness of man's venture in its unusual architecture. Earth is mounded around the frame of the building; a huge 56-foot dome covers the theatre.

A stop here—the museum is open March through November—reveals everything your amateur astronauts ever wanted to know about mankind's venture into air and space. Seven galleries are filled with vintage aircraft and spacecraft exhibits as well as artifacts such as moon rocks, model airplane collections, Armstrong's spacesuit, and samples of space food. A cubic room of mirrors simulates the vastness of space, and the Astro-Theater has multimedia space shows.

Other must-see highlights include the *Toledo II,* the first manned and powered airship to grace the New York City skies; the *Gemini VIII* spacecraft flown by Armstrong in 1966; a model of the *Saturn V* rocket and the Astro-Theater, which features a multimedia presentation of the sights and sounds of space against a starry sky. The annual **Festival of Flight,** held in mid-July, includes a model rocket launch, a HAM radio demonstration, airplane shows, food, and games. Admission is $4.00 for adults; $1.00 for children ages three to twelve. For more information call (419) 738–8811.

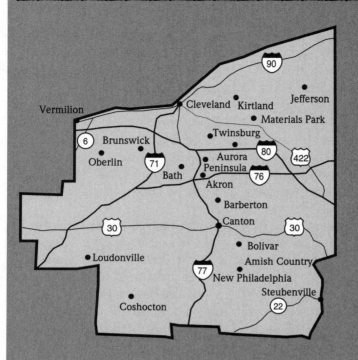

Vermilion

Cleveland · Kirtland

· Jefferson

· Materials Park

6 · Brunswick

· Twinsburg

· Oberlin

71 · Aurora
Peninsula

80 422

· Bath

76

Akron

· Barberton

Canton

30 30

· Bolivar

· Loudonville

· Amish Country

77 New Philadelphia

Steubenville

· Coshocton

22

Northeast Ohio

NORTHEAST OHIO

Northeast Ohio has an eclectic flavor all its own, from sleepy fishing villages reminiscent of America's East Coast and relaxing Lake Erie getaways to bustling big cities and Major League excitement. With the recent opening of the Cleveland Rock 'n' Roll Museum, this region proves that it really shakes, rattles, and rolls. And, if that weren't enough, your family can take in the World's Largest Tooth in Cleveland, rub noses with marine mammals at Sea World in Aurora, tackle history at the Pro Football Hall of Fame in Canton, or hitch a ride on a horse-drawn buggy through Amish Country. It's all here.

VERMILION

Tiny sailors can grab a steamer's helm or explore an authentic pilothouse as they imagine themselves navigating the mighty Great Lakes at the **Inland Seas Maritime Museum.** This charming lakeside town—one of the first you encounter as you skirt Lake Erie and enter Northeast Ohio—is home to one of the few museums celebrating life on the historic waterways known as the Great Lakes.

Pore over shipwright models, newspapers, photographs, and artifacts that capture the Golden Age of Great Lakes maritime history. Wander among vintage photographs, instruments, hands-on tools, and displays that tell the history of the Battle of Lake Erie. There are also timbers from the *Niagara* (Admiral Perry's 1812 flagship), a video that recounts the wreck of the *Edmund Fitzgerald,* and a well-stocked gift shop with books and mementos of Great Lakes life. Hours are daily from 10:00 A.M. to 5:00 P.M.; admission is $4.00 for adults, $3.00 for seniors, and $2.00 for students under age sixteen.

Adjacent is the classic **Vermilion Lighthouse** built in 1847, rebuilt in 1859, and finished in 1877. A 400-foot catwalk ran parallel to a concrete pier, linking the lighthouse to the mainland. The brave keeper used this walkway to reach the light whenever waves crested over the pier. When the lighthouse began tilting toward the busy harbor in 1929, it was dismantled by a group of concerned citizens. In 1992 it was rebuilt yet again. Today its rare 1891 Fresnel lens serves as a nighttime messenger once more. For more information on the museum or lighthouse call (216) 967–3467.

Don't leave the area without sampling the filling fare at **Sal & Al's Diner** in Amherst, east of Vermilion. You'll be movin' and groovin' to the beat of an old-style jukebox as you feast on a menu loaded with 1950s favorites—all made from scratch—such as hot roast beef with mashed potatoes and gravy, barbecued pork sandwich, burgers 'n' fries, and BLTs. Afterward get a lick in at **George's Tin Roof** ice cream parlor, which is adjacent. The restaurant is at 2261 Cooper Foster Park Road; call (216) 282–4367.

OBERLIN

Ohio and its residents played a key part in the African-American struggle for freedom prior to and during the Civil War. Some 50,000 to 75,000 fugitive slaves passed through the state on the Underground Railroad; during this time, dozens of "railroad lines" stretched from the banks of the Ohio River to the shores of Lake Erie.

Although former stations exist in virtually all regions of the state, few are as significant as Lorain County and the town of Oberlin, which has a specially designed **African-American Heritage Tour** available through the Lorain County Visitors Bureau. Oberlin gained notoriety as "the town that started the Civil War when it harbored fugitive John Price during what later became known as the Oberlin–Wellington Slave Rescue of 1858.

Plaques now mark some of the famous rescue sites. In Oberlin many of the rescuers are buried in Westwood Cemetery, and many of the churches involved in the rescue, including the First Church of Oberlin, the meeting site for the Oberlin Antislavery Society, still stand. Don't miss the moving **Underground Railroad Memorial.** Oberlin is also home to **Oberlin College,** the first American college to admit students "irrespective of color" in 1835. Your kids may eschew the textbooks, but a visit here will bring history to vivid, moving life in a lesson they'll long remember. For more information contact the Lorain County Visitors Bureau at (800) 334-1673.

CLEVELAND

Ohio's second largest city, once jokingly referred to as the "mistake by the lake" is having the last laugh these days. Around the country urban planners and envious city officials are pointing to Cleveland as the comeback city of the century.

Today, it's also a sophisticated metropolis and a fascinating family destination. Despite an industrial bent, you'll find more than 19,000 acres of parkland and 90 miles of scenic Lake Erie shoreline, one of the country's finest art museums, and a renowned group of professional theaters for playgoers of all ages. Clevelanders are proud of their city, a five-time recipient of the prestigious All-American City Award, most recently in 1993. For more on current events, weekend packages, and theater tickets, call the handy Visitor Information Hotline at (800) 321-1004.

Visitors throughout 1996 are invited to join in the exciting **Cleveland Bicentennial festivities** and even sign a giant birthday card donated by American Greetings that will travel around the city. A yearlong bash is planned to commemorate the city's founding by Moses Cleaveland, a representative of the Connecticut Land Company. Cleaveland led a plucky band of pioneers looking to settle the land westward and founded the area now known as Cleveland on July 22, 1796.

Events include a festive New Year's Eve "First Weekend" kickoff with indoor and outdoor performances; a gala, citywide birthday party in July, with a spectacular waterfront celebration; and a fall "Homecoming" for all current and former Clevelanders (and, of course, guests). Area attractions will get in the act as well as a special yearlong program of exhibits and performances. For more information on the bicentennial events call (216) 961-1996 or (216) 771-4070.

KHRISTI'S TOP FAMILY ADVENTURES IN NORTHEAST OHIO

1. Sea World, Aurora
2. Amish Country
3. Twins Days Festival, Twinsburg
4. Quaker Square, Akron
5. Rock 'n' Roll Hall of Fame, Cleveland

Any time you visit, a good way to get a handle on Cleveland's many offerings is to take one of the old-fashioned one- or two-hour **Trolley Tours** of downtown. Climb aboard one of five nostalgic bright red trolleys, complete with carved oak interior, wrought iron seat decoration, and the requisite clanging bell and take in more than 20 miles of scenic stops and more than 100 sights. All of the trolleys are appropriately nicknamed "Lolly" (the company also owns Gus and Russ the Bus, Stan the Sedan, and Dan the Van). Tickets range from $5.00 to $10.00 depending on the tour. Tours leave from Burke Lakefront Airport on North Marginal Road downtown. For tickets and information call (216) 771–4484.

If you and your family are sailors, you might prefer getting your feet wet aboard the cruises offered by the triple-deck, 1,000-passenger *Goodtime III,* the city's largest sightseeing charter boat. Two-hour excursions depart daily at 1:00 and 3:30 P.M. and take in all the city sights along the river and lake.

Don't forget to bring your camera. You'll enjoy a fast-changing panorama of vistas and views as the skyline passes. Tickets are $8.95 per person. There are also popular dinner and dinner-dance cruises. For information call (216) 861–5110. Sightseeing cruises are also offered by the elegant *Nautica Queen,* which offers daily lunch and dinner departures as well as a Sunday brunch. Most families opt for the popular luncheon cruise on Saturdays, featuring a groaning-board buffet of beef or chicken entree, pasta Alfredo, pasta marinara, dessert, mixed greens, and more. Prices are $16.95 per person; $9.95 for kids age twelve and under. For reservations call (216) 696–8888. Both cruises operate April through October, weather permitting.

Steamship lovers can climb aboard the **William G. Mather Museum** for another look at life on the high seas. The former flagship of the Cleveland Cliffs Iron Company is docked at downtown's East Ninth Street Pier and is now a floating discovery center. At 618 feet, it was built in 1925 to carry ore, coal, and grain throughout the Great Lakes but now houses exhibits and displays that focus on the history and lore of these "iron boats." Would-be sailors are escorted through the pilothouse, the crew and guest quarters, the galley, as well as the guest and officers' dining room. A favorite of most kids is the huge, four-story engine room. Tours are offered daily from June through August and on weekends in May, September, and October. For more information call (216) 574–6262.

Prefer to go *under* the water? Indulge your undersea adventurers with a visit to the **USS Cod,** docked at North Marginal Road near the Burke Lakefront Airport. This World War II submarine—the last original and intact model left from a one-time fleet of more than 200—offers a real submarine-style experience. The 312-foot *Cod* is credited with seven successful war patrols that sank more than 27,000 tons of Imperial Japanese shipping. When it was retired from reserve training in 1976, it was saved from the scrap pile by a dedicated group of local veterans. Visitors are taken through the submarine's eight compartments, given demonstrations on its works, as well a lively history of life on board. Tickets are $4.00 for adults, $2.00 for children. For more information call (216) 566–8770.

If you opt to explore the city via your own two feet, better first put on your dancing shoes. Your first stop should be the new **Rock 'n' Roll Museum** downtown. Located along Cleveland's North Coast Harbor (not far from where the *Goodtime III* is docked), this stunning design includes a 165-foot tower that rises from the water and a variety of geometric shapes that explode from the tower, along with a shimmering, seven-story triangular-shaped glass tent.

Boogie on over and get ready to rock around the clock. After a national competition and years of planning, the 150,000-square-foot hall of fame and museum opened in September 1995. Internationally acclaimed architect I. M. Pei (known for his controversial addition to the Louvre Museum in Paris) designed the museum to be as groundbreaking and far-reaching as the musical style it honors.

City fathers claimed that Cleveland was the most appropriate place all along, since legendary disc jockey Alan Freed coined the phrase "Rock 'n' Roll" here during a 1951 broadcast. The city also served as the site of the first rock concert, the Moon Dog Coronation Ball, held in 1952.

Organizers hope to tell the story of rock 'n' roll from its roots in country, blues, R&B, and jazz to the latest forms of hip-hop and rap. Among the more than 4,000 artifacts in the collection are Elvis Presley's black leather outfit, worn in his 1968 TV special; John Lennon's "Sgt. Pepper's Lonely Hearts Club Band" uniform; original recording equipment from Sun Studios in Memphis; handwritten lyrics by Chuck Berry and Jimmy Hendrix; Jim Morrison's Cub Scout uniform; Roy Orbison's sunglasses; and more.

This may seem like ancient history to your kids, but they can't help but be excited by the exhibits that let them host a live radio broadcast, or see the recording booths that show how hit songs are created and recorded. The 50,000-square feet of exhibit space also feature lively displays and memorabilia (but be forewarned: Your young music fans won't be able to resist poking fun at the way things were when you were young). More recent groups (and those more recognizable to young fans), such as Irish rockers U2 and rapper Queen Latifah, are also included.

The Rock 'n' Roll Hall of Fame is at 1 Key Plaza in Cleveland. For more information call (216) 781–7625.

Just steps away is the new $54.9 million, 165,000-square-foot **Great Lakes Science Center,** also located on the section of Lake Erie known as the North Coast Harbor. When it opens in summer 1996, it will be one of the most innovative science centers in the world.

Designed to provide a comprehensive learning center, it will feature 50,000 square feet of exciting hands-on exhibits that encourage young and old visitors alike to have fun while they learn. Features include a 20,000-square-foot gallery devoted to traveling and seasonal exhibits, an intriguing S.E.T. Piece, which concentrates on major themes of science, environment, and technology, a huge 320-seat Omnimax Theater, and another sure-hit: a riveting replica of the NASA mission control station in Houston. For more information call (216) 736–7900.

The waterfront is also home to the **Flats,** a restored area located not far away along the Cleveland Memorial Shoreway. Once the home of hundreds of heavy industries, the Flats is now the city's premier entertainment district. An interesting mix of converted warehouses dots the east and west banks of the area where the Cuyahoga River meets Lake Erie. The popular **Nautica Entertainment Complex** covers some twenty-eight acres on the river's west bank and includes an amphitheater, a riverfront boardwalk, and a floating restaurant. Anchored by two dramatic jackknife bridges, the complex has attracted millions of people since it opened in 1987. Pig out on pasta at the **Spaghetti Warehouse,** a family favorite. You can even dine in a trolley car. Afterward, if your offspring are into sing-alongs, buy them a soda and check out the fun at the rollicking **Howl at the Moon Saloon.** Dueling baby grands and TV theme songs make this a popular spot with teenagers and college students.

The complex is also home to the popular **Cleveland Cool KidsFest,** an outdoor festival just for kids that's held each July. Special entertainment, sports, rides, activities, games, and more make up this weekend of fun for all ages. For more information call (216) 247–2722.

The district really heats up at night, when the nightclubs host big-name entertainment from all over the country, but it's a pleasant place for a family *al fresco* lunch anytime and a great spot to watch passing freighters, some of which reach up to 600 feet long and fly flags from all over the world. Even landlubbers love listening to the freighters boom their horn blasts of greeting as they pass each other. It's also home to the city's rowing clubs, which can be seen in warmer months. The Flats Racing League now has more than 1,200 members.

Another great place for an impromptu and always fresh meal is the historic **West Side Market,** located at West Twenty-Fifth Street and Lorain Avenue. Duck inside the door of this vintage 1912 Old-World-style market—one of the largest and last in the United States—and you'll be overwhelmed by the smells of exotic meats and cheeses, fresh baked goods, and more. More than 100 indoor and outdoor merchants from a variety of ethnic groups serve up anything your family's hearts desire in a friendly, carnival-type setting. Not surprisingly, kids often opt for a hot dog—some of the best in the city—from one of the many vendors. Chocoholics of all ages are in for a treat in Cleveland. Two local candy companies—**Malley's Chocolates** in Cleveland and **Olympia Gourmet Chocolates and Corn** in nearby suburban Strongsville—offer tours and, of course, free samples of their gooey goodies. At Malley's you'll hear the story of chocolate, see nuts roasted, chocolates dipped, molds filled, and fancy packages wrapped. The factory is at 13400 Brookpark Road; call (800) 835-5684.

Ever see the episode of the "I Love Lucy" show when Lucy does a stint at a chocolate factory? Don a hair net, apron, and surgical gloves and see for yourself what it's like at Olympia Gourmet Chocolates. Olympia, which has been around for more than eighty years, specializes in gourmet chocolate candy and caramel corn. Visitors get in the action during the two-hour tours and help make their signature chocolate goodies. Afterward, you can fill up a box with your favorite creations. Tours are $10.00 for adults, $5.00 for kids, and include a box of chocolate and a bag of caramel corn. Tours are offered depending on demand; reservations are necessary. Olympia is at 15155 Pearl Road, Strongsville; call (800) 574-7747.

If you're a family of sports lovers, Cleveland is your town. From the statewide Browns–Bengals rivalry to the excitement of a buzzer shot at a Cavs game, Cleveland offers enough thrills to satisfy sportsaholics of any age.

Catch an Indians game at the new **Jacobs Field** in the heart of downtown. This state-of-the-art facility holds 42,000 screaming fans who come to experience the thrills of America's favorite pastime while enjoying spectacular views of the field, skyline, and the largest freestanding scoreboard in North America.

Jacobs Field is part of the city's world-class sports and entertainment complex that opened in 1994. Located downtown on the site of the twenty-eight-acre Old Central Market, **Gateway Ballpark and Arena** has gained international attention for the visionary design and its two arenas— the aforementioned $161 million, 42,200-seat Jacobs Field and an $118 million, 20,750-seat indoor arena, home of the Cleveland Cavaliers NBA basketball team, the Lumberjacks hockey team, the Thunderbolts Arena football team, as well as concerts and family-oriented special events. The ballpark is a mere five-minute stroll from most downtown hotels and is connected by a walkway to Tower City Center. With panoramic views of the city's skyline, a restaurant that looks out over the playing field, food courts, and tempting team gift shops—as well as a collection of colorful public art by noted regional artists, Gateway is sure to score with fans.

Although sports are a big ticket in Cleveland, many visitors are surprised to discover that the arts draw even larger crowds. While professional sports brought in $79 million in the early 1990s, the arts added some $190.5 million to the city's coffers.

Of those art lovers, nearly 25 percent lined up for the city's live theater. Cleveland is considered Broadway's home away from home, with many major shows either debuting or coproduced here. Recent productions have included *Phantom Of The Opera, Grease,* and the family favorite, *The Nutcracker.* It's a great place to introduce your offspring to the roar of the greasepaint without the sticker shock you'll find these days on the Great White Way, where good seats can easily cost $75.

The cornerstone of Cleveland theater is **Playhouse Square,** now the third-largest performing arts center in the country, with more than 7,000 seats and nearly a million annual patrons of all ages. Playhouse Square boasts four renovated theaters, all of which are worth visiting for a tour even if nothing's on stage.

The spectacular Ohio, State, Palace, and Allen Theaters, all of which were originally built in the 1920s as vaudeville palaces, were converted in the 1950s to movie houses and fell into disrepair in the late 1960s. After a long fund-raising drive, Playhouse Square became home to five resident companies, including the Cleveland Opera, the Cleveland Ballet, the Ohio Ballet, Dance-Cleveland, and the Great Lakes Theater Festival. The Great Lakes Theater Festival was established in 1961 to preserve classic theater—one of only a few companies left in the United States dedicated to this form. Performances range from *A Christmas Carol* to *A Midsummer Night's Dream.*

Another long-standing Cleveland theatrical tradition is the **Cleveland Playhouse.** Founded in 1915, it's the oldest nonprofit professional theater in the country and specializes in producing favorites as well as original plays.

Also founded in 1915, the **Karamu House** is the oldest African-American theater in the country. The theater pioneered interracial theater in its early days and featured the works of many unknown black playwrights.

Are your kids budding playwrights? Last, but not least, each year the city's **Dobama Theater** features the annual, award-winning **Marilyn Bianchi Kids' Playwrighting Festival,** the first arts festival in the country in which a resident company performs plays written by children from elementary through high school.

The arts also take center stage in **University Circle,** about 4 miles east of downtown. Just one mile long, the area is home to internationally renowned museums; performing arts centers; music, art, and educational institutions—the largest concentration in the country. All are within walking distance of one another and situated in a relaxing parklike setting of manicured gardens and winding boulevards.

Nearby is the **Cleveland Health Education Museum.** Stop yawning; this fascinating, forty-thousand-square-foot museum is a kid's favorite and the first museum of its kind in America. The more than 200 permanent exhibits include Juno, the talking transparent woman; the world's largest tooth, which towers above your heads at 18 feet; the family discovery center; and the theaters of Hearing, Sight, and Social Concerns. If you've never been able to address the question of the birds and the bees, don't miss the section called the Wonder of New Life, which tells the reproduction story in an easy-to-understand cartoon style. The museum is at 8911 Euclid Avenue; for information call (216) 231–5010.

Ominous-looking swords, halberds, daggers, and suits of armor are a longtime favorite of young visitors to the **Cleveland Museum of Art,** also on University Circle. Other top choices in this three-story classical structure include the Wishing Well in the Indoor Garden Court, the Egyptian galleries, the African and Oceanic galleries, and the large Guardian figures at the entrance to the Asian galleries. Check out the whimsical animal-shaped tea set by designer Carlo Bugatti in the sculpture, decorative arts, and textiles area; the painted African masks in the African galleries; or try and find the violin in Pablo Picasso's *Harlequin with Violin*. Richard Stankiewicz's *Untitled* sculpture may inspire young recyclers to go home and create a sculpture using cans and other throwaways.

But there's certainly more to this renowned museum than ancient weapons of war. With more than 30,000 works of art spanning more than 5,000 years, there's something to suit every taste. The museum was founded by a group of civic-minded philanthropists "for the benefit of all the people forever" and opened to the public in 1916. True to the spirit of the founders, general admission is always free—one of the few museums across the country to remain so.

Mom and Dad can join in the free fun on the third Sunday of every month during Family Express, a hands-on activity designed for the whole gang. No advance registration is required, and participants can come and go as they please. Another popular series is the Young People's Classes, where young art enthusiasts observe the collection and make their own works of art inspired by those studied. The museum is one of the few that allow hands-on projects to be made in the galleries—under strict supervision, of course. Classes are offered for preschool- through high-school-age children.

The Cleveland Museum of Art is at 11150 East Boulevard. Hours are 10:00 A.M. to 5:45 P.M. Tuesday, Thursday, and Friday; 10:00 A.M. to 9:00 P.M. Wednesday; 9:00 A.M. to 4:45 P.M. Saturday; and 1:00 to 5:45 P.M. Sunday. For more information contact (216) 421–0411.

"Please Touch" could be the motto of the innovative **Cleveland Children's Museum** on Euclid Avenue in University Circle. More like an activity center than a museum, it houses more than 100 displays that the whole gang can enjoy. Get wet—or at least learn about the properties of water—at "Water, Water Everywhere," which explores the mysteries of water and its cycles as children pour and pump, carve riverbanks, work waterwheels, draw fish, and enjoy racing a boat along a replica of Lake Erie.

Prefer heights? Enter a deep forest to check out "Tales in Tall Trees," which encourages storymaking and an understanding of the role of storytelling in many cultures. A maze, puppets, dioramas, and a gallery of wild beasts are just a few of the things on hand to foster wonder, imagination, and play. Other "old favorites" include the "Over and Under Bridges" area, where child-sized bridges can be worked by little hands, and the popular "People Puzzle" that lets kids create their own self-portrait, compare diverse features, play with puppets, and try their hand a being a roving reporter.

The museum is open 11:00 A.M. to 5:00 P.M. Monday through Friday

TOP ANNUAL EVENTS IN NORTHEAST OHIO

Pro Football Festival, July, Canton; (216) 456–8207
Twins Days Festival, August, Twinsburg; (216) 425–3652
All-American Soap Box Derby, August, Akron; (216) 733–8723
Great Mohican Indian Pow-Wow and Rendezvous, September,
    Loudonville; (419) 994–4008
Ohio Swiss Festival, September, Sugar Creek; (216) 852–3252
Covered Bridge Festival, October, Jefferson; (216) 576–3769
Apple Butter Stirrin', October, Coshocton; (800) 877–1830

from mid-June through Labor Day; hours vary during the school year. For more information call (216) 791–KIDS.

Want to have light-years of fun in a single day? Head for the **Cleveland Museum of Natural History,** Ohio's largest natural science museum, also located in University Circle. The Barney set loves the dinosaurs and other prehistoric creatures, as well as the birds, botany and geology exhibits, and the fascinating Hall of Man, home to "Lucy," the three-million-year-old skeleton of the oldest known human.

Regarded as one of the finest in North America, the museum is housed in a modern, 200,000-square-foot facility and draws 400,000 visitors annually. Many came to see the Foucault Pendulum in the main lobby, which demonstrates the rotation of the earth. It's the world's only pendulum in which the electromagnet that keeps the 270-lb. bob moving is placed underneath rather than mounted on the top.

Rock hounds of all ages appreciate the Gem Room, with an impressive collection of quartz crystals, opals, and diamonds in a rainbow of colors (the museum has more than 30,000 specimens). Kids of all interests ooh and aah at "Happy," the skeleton of the 70-foot-long haplocanthosaurus, one of the oldest sauropods on display anywhere in the world. See stars in the state's oldest planetarium, and come nose to nose with native animals and wildlife in the outdoor environmental courtyard or rustic wood garden. Browse in the well-stocked gift shop, cleverly named the "Ark In The Park."

The museum is open from 10:00 A.M. to 5:00 P.M. Monday through Saturday and Wednesday evenings until 10:00 P.M. (September through May). Admission is $6.00 for adults; $4.00 for children ages five to seventeen and seniors; free on Tuesdays and Thursdays from 3:00 to 5:00 P.M. The museum is located at 1 Wade Oval Drive; for information call (216) 231–4600.

History of another kind lives on at the **Western Reserve Historical Society,** Cleveland's oldest cultural institution. It was founded in 1867 to preserve and promote the area's rich heritage.

Baseball, roller coasters, classic cars, bowling machines, airplanes, log cabins, and more are crammed into this collection that captures the area's diverse past. Browse among the costumes, farming tools, manuscripts, and period rooms that recreate the area known as the Western Reserve from the pre-Revolutionary War era through the early twentieth century.

Centerpiece of the museum is the Hay–McKinney mansion, built in 1911 and designed by the son of President James Garfield. The ornate Italian Florentine-style villa is filled with important period furniture, decorative arts, and once was part of the city's "Millionaires' Row" that stretched along part of Euclid Avenue (the mayor's home located here even boasted an indoor ice-skating rink). Tours also take you "downstairs" to the servant's quarters for a starkly different view of nineteenth-century life.

Car buffs of all ages flock to the society's **Crawford Auto–Aviation Museum,** which houses more than 150 streamlined, vintage and classic automobiles and aircraft, including a rare collection of Cleveland-built cars. Especially popular with little (and big!) boys, it's considered one of the finest collections in the nation. Girls get equal time at the Chisholm Halle Costume Wing, where kids' clothes, men's suits, hats, shoes, and more encourage dress-up fantasies and make the wing the best-dressed tourist attraction in town. Everyone likes a stroll down the re-created turn-of-the-century "Street of Shops."

The Western Reserve Historical Society is open 10:00 A.M. to 5:00 P.M. Tuesday through Saturday; noon to 5:00 P.M. Sunday; closed Monday. It's located at 10825 East Boulevard; call (216) 721–5722 for information. You can't go far these days without seeing a bumper sticker that says "Save The Rain Forest." The folks at the **Cleveland MetroParks Zoo** have taken these sentiments a step further with the opening of the groundbreaking RainForest exhibition three years ago.

After eight years of planning and nearly $30 million in expenses, this tropical netherworld opened in 1992. Under a domed, copper-colored glass structure that covers two floors and some 80,000 square feet, the RainForest gives refuge to more than 600 animals from more than 118 species that are in the process of losing or have lost their natural habitat. There are also more than 10,000 plants from 360 different varieties and sixty-five different plant families housed here.

In many ways, it's like a modern-day Noah's Ark. There are small-clawed otters, ocelots, dwarf crocodiles, golden lion monkeys, Puerto Rican crested toads, and even Dumeril ground boas. Many of the species found here have never been seen at the zoo.

As you wander along paths lined with low, leafy plants and orchid-studded trees, a continuous soundtrack plays recordings made in real rain forests. Nearby, a 30-foot indoor waterfall pours 90,000 gallons of recycled water per minute, sending beads of water into air that is already kept at an eighty degree temperature with 80 percent humidity. The climax of your visit is a series of rain-forest storms, complete with heart-pounding thunder, blinding lightning, and overhead rain. You can't help but be moved as you watch a video of bulldozers and chain saws tear away at the soil near the exhibition's exit.

While the RainForest is a popular attraction, the zoo is also home to more than 3,000 other animals, birds, and fish living in simulated natural habitats. You'll see ostriches, zebras, and giraffes in Africa; and sharks, lungfish, and piranhas in the aquatics area. Kangaroos and wallabies populate the lands known as Australasia, where you can hop on the Outback Railroad for a tour. Other highlights include the Birds of Prey, the Public Greenhouse, and the Rhinoceros/Cheetah area. The zoo is open daily from 9:00 A.M. to 5:00 P.M.; the RainForest is open daily from 10:00 A.M. to 5:00

P.M. Admission is $7.00 for adults; $4.00 for ages two to eleven. For more information call (216) 661–6500.

Don't leave Cleveland without getting an eagle's-eye view of the city from on top of the forty-second floor of the Terminal Tower in **Tower City Center.** From the Observation Deck you can see all of Cleveland spread out before you, from high-rises and concrete to surrounding suburbs, to the ever-present blue expanse of the Lake Erie shoreline. Tickets are $2.00 for adults, $1.00 for children (free for kids under age five) and can be purchased at the Tower City Center Visitors Information Center. The deck is open daily in summer from 11:00 A.M. to 3:30 P.M. and weekends all other months from 11:00 A.M. to 4:30 P.M. For more information call (216) 621–7981.

You'll also get a head rush from a visit to the **NASA Lewis Research Center,** not far from the airport, where the "final frontier" is the focus. It's up, up, and away at one of the country's most advanced research facilities, one of just ten such centers in the United States and the only one in the Midwest.

With programs in aeronautics and space-age technology, NASA Lewis is also home to the Microgravity Materials Science Laboratory, a facility used to test potential space experiments, a zero-gravity drop tower, wind tunnels, space environment tanks, and chambers for testing jet-engine efficiency and noise.

All this and more is explored in a fascinating 8,000-square-foot Visitors Center. Here, amateur astronauts head for the authentic Apollo/Skylab capsule, the Lunar Lander computer game, and various other exhibits tracing the history of space exploration. The center opened its doors to the public in 1976 and has welcomed more than 100,000 visitors each year since.

In eight exhibition galleries you'll find a variety of educational and informative programs on Aeronautics, Space Exploration, the Solar System, Air and Spacecraft Propulsion, the Space Shuttle and the Apollo Skylab III Command Module, Satellites, Materials and Structures Research, and Spinoffs of NASA programs. A popular lecture series focuses on topics related to aeronautics, such as "Space Basics 101" and "Fostering Your Daughter's Enjoyment and Success in Math, Science, and Engineering." The auditorium features special videos related to recent NASA shuttle missions. Across from the Visitors Center you'll also find large examples of the 15,775-pound Agena Rocket; the 800-lb. Ranger, designed to broadcast pictures from the moon; and Centaur Rocket, used on planetary and satellite launches since 1966.

If your kids are teenagers, consider the insider's view of the research center's activities offered on Wednesday afternoons from 2:00 to 3:00 P.M. (no one under age 16 is admitted, and proof of citizenship is required). Tours visit the flight research building, the propulsion systems lab, the zero-gravity facility and the ten-by-ten-foot supersonic wind tunnel. Reservations must be made ahead of time.

NASA Lewis Research Center is at 21000 Brookpark Road; it's free and open 9:00 A.M. to 4:00 P.M. weekdays; 10:00 A.M. to 3:00 P.M. Saturdays; and 1:00 to 5:00 P.M. Sundays. For more information call (216) 433–2001.

KIRTLAND

A little science. A little history. A lot of fun.

The brochure for **Lake Farm Park,** an open-air science and cultural center just east of downtown Cleveland, says it all. With 235 acres of fields and forests, more than fifty breeds of livestock (including more than a dozen endangered breeds), wagon and sleigh rides, and more, it's a city kid's country fantasy come true.

Teach your horticulturalists or farmers-to-be with a visit to the hydroponic greenhouse displays or the strange-but-wonderful "Great Tomato Works," billed as "the world's most unusual horticultural science exhibit."

The Great Tomato Works includes the world's largest tomato hornworm and the world's largest tomato plant, with vines as big as your waist, fruit 6 feet across and leaves up to 12 feet long. The display also explores the life processes of plants and food production, including hands-on exhibits that show how plants make sugar from sunshine, how roots store water, and how wild tomatoes are transformed into ketchup.

The farm is also the spot for fun at year-round festivals, including the Woolly World Fest in May, a Fall Harvest in September, and the ever-popular Farmpark Sheepdog Challenge in November. Afterward, stop for a bite at the Calf-A restaurant.

The Farm Park is located at 8800 Chardon Road and is open year-round from 9:00 A.M. to 5:00 P.M. daily; closed Monday January through March. For more information call (216) 256–2122 or (800) 366–FARM.

Looking to get back to nature? Kirtland is also home to the largest arboretum in the United States. **Holden Arboretum** is a 3,100-acre preserve of natural woodlands, horticultural collections, display gardens, walking trails, ponds, and open fields. Plants include rhododendrons, crab apple, maples, conifers, nut trees, wildflowers, lilacs, and viburnums.

This is a great place to wind down and explore the wilderness. After a stop at the informative Visitors Center, take to the trails or enjoy an *al fresco* meal at the scenic picnic area on the grounds. Self-guided tours are available Tuesday through Sunday from 10:00 A.M. to 5:00 P.M.; guided tours are offered by reservation. Admission is $2.50 for adults, $1.75 for ages six to fifteen. For more information call (216) 946–4400.

Need to cool off? The new kid on the block in Lake County is the **Fairport Harbor Lakefront Beach Park.** This twenty-acre, $1.6 million beach is definitely worth a stop—and a dip. Stock up on the sunscreen, and load up the picnic basket—you'll find long stretches of sandy beach, concession stands, playgrounds, picnic areas, and water-equipment rental, even a lighthouse museum. For more information call (800) 227–PARK.

JEFFERSON

Continue to skirt Lake Erie and eventually you'll end up in Ashtabula County, best known as the covered bridge capital of Ohio. Who needs Madison County when Ashtabula has a record fifteen covered bridges of its own?

From the Creek Road Covered Bridge, which has an unknown date of construction, to Harpersfield Covered Bridge, the longest in the state of Ohio and a designated National Historic Site, Ashtabula is proud of its bridges and heritage. So proud, in fact, that they now have a **Covered Bridge Festival** each year on the second weekend in October.

Antique engines and tractors, a Civil War encampment, a parade, and covered bridge tours are just a few of the highlights. Children love the scarecrow contest, the Ding-a-Ling Train Rides, the draft horse pull, plowing contest, and lively entertainment. Admission is $2.00 for adults; free for children age 12 and younger. For more information contact the festival office at 25 West Jefferson Street or call (216) 576–3769.

Covered bridges are so much a part of the area psyche that there's even a pizza parlor in one. In 1972 Ashtabula County sold one of its covered bridges—formerly known as the Forman Road Bridge—for just $5.00. Today it's known as **Covered Bridge Pizza,** and located both in neighboring Kingsville and in Andover. Dine in the bridge built in 1862 and enjoy homemade pizza, pasta, chili, sandwiches, and subs. The restaurants are at 380 East Main Street in Andover (216–293–6776); and Route 193, North Kingsville (216–224–0497).

Afterward, make your way along historic Ashtabula Harbor to the **Great Lakes Marine and U.S. Coast Guard Memorial Museum,** where you can explore Great Lakes history. The small but charming museum is housed in the old lighthouse keeper's home, a duplex built in 1898. The U.S. Coast Guard took it over and used it as a station before it became a volunteer-run museum in 1984. Today you can explore the seven rooms and a pilothouse from a 1911 *Thomas Walters,* an ore boat built in nearby Lorain. Small fry especially like the working radar and the rare working model of a hulett, an iron ore unloading machine. Only four are left standing on Lake Erie today. There are also photographs, clothing, and other mementos of a sailor's life on the lake. Hours are noon to 6:00 P.M. Friday, Saturday, and Sunday in summer, and 1:00 to 5:00 P.M. till the end of October. The museum is at 1071 Walnut Boulevard; for information call (216) 964–6847.

TWINSBURG

Don't blink . . . there's nothing wrong with your eyes. You'll be seeing lots of doubles during the annual **Twins Days Festival,** the largest gathering of twins in the world. Even the town, located along I–480 about midway between Cleveland and Akron, was named after the more than 1,500 sets of identical and fraternal twins who congregate here the first full weekend in August each year. The festival was founded in 1976 as part of the city of Twinsburg's bicentennial festivities and commemorates town founders Moses and Aaron Wilcox, twin brothers who settled the town in the early 1800s.

This prime people-watching weekend has been featured in *Newsweek, Reader's Digest, People Magazine,* and on the ABC "World News Tonight." It's featured in the *Guinness Book of World Records* as the largest gathering of twins. It's grown from just thirty-seven sets of twins in 1976 to almost 3,000 in 1995. But you and your family don't have to have a double to enjoy the festival. Events include the "Double-Take Parade," chock-full of twins, floats, and marching bands. Each day, twins participate in more than thirty-five twins contests, including most or least identical, oldest, youngest, farthest traveled, even widest combined smile! Besides all this, there's a wide variety of arts and crafts, rides for kids, games, food stands, exhibits, and entertainment. Other highlights include a twin fireworks display, group photos (there are so many attendees that they take them on a hill near the town), and more. Admission is a bargain at just a buck per person, including parking. For more information contact the Twins Days Festival Committee, Inc., P.O. Box 29, Twinsburg, 44807 or call (216) 425–3652.

AURORA

Mention the area around Cleveland to most kids, and their first question is "Isn't that by **Sea World?**" This wet and wonderful marine-life park—known nationally as the home of Shamu, the killer whale—is a family favorite and a must-see. Other Sea Worlds exist across the country, but this one, located between Cleveland and Akron, is the only one in the Midwest.

Where else can you touch the cool, rubbery skin of a dolphin, come nose to nose with a shark, enjoy a close encounter with a tuxedoed penguin, toss a tasty treat to a seal, or thrill to one of seven live shows? With ninety acres of lush, rolling hills and oceans of fun, Sea World offers visitors an unparalleled journey into the world of the sea.

The year 1995 was a busy one for the popular park. New features include the interactive Dolphin Cove, where visitors step into the underwater world of the bottlenose dolphin. A dozen delightful dolphins cavort in the 375,000-gallon environment while their humanlike "talking" is amplified by underwater microphones. America's national bird gets its due at the recently opened Eagle Point, where rehabilitated bald eagles from the World Bird Sanctuary make their home in a re-creation of a North American woodland setting. Like silly shows? Check out the always-hilarious antics of performing sea lions Clyde and Seamore.

And that's just the beginning. The park's longtime favorite attractions include Shark Encounter, the Midwest's largest shark display, where a moving walkway travels under huge curved tanks and puts you face to face with these incredible but often misunderstood animals; the colorful "World Of The Sea" aquarium, with twenty geographically themed areas and a Hawaiian Tide Pool, where kids can examine starfish and sea urchins; and the Killer Whale and Dolphin Show, where families crowd the lower seats to be sure of getting drenched.

Afterward, let your little marine biologists cool down at Shamu's Happy Harbor, a colorful three-acre Caribbean-themed adventure land for children, complete with palm trees and giant pink flamingos. Here they can climb a 50-foot-high, four-story net with 40,000 feet of netting, eighteen tunnels and a suspended submarine; negotiate a splashy water maze; slip down nine slippery slides; lose their allowance in the Coco Loco Arcade; or bury themselves in thousands of colorful plastic balls.

For a different view of the park, consider visiting after 6:00 P.M., when guests can save up to $7.00 on admission (that adds up with a big family). You'll enjoy all of the park's regular attractions and be dazzled as they turn out the lights and put on an incredible laser, movie, and outdoor fireworks extravaganza.

Although entertainment is a large part of Sea World's mission, the park is also committed to education, conservation, and research. The park assists in the rehabilitation of rescued animals, provides information for the protection of Ohio's native fishes, establishes breeding and research programs, and works to educate the public on environmental issues through their exhibits and educational offerings.

Sea World is open from May through September. Admission is $23.95 for adults (ages 12 and older); $18.95 for children ages three to eleven; younger than three free. Open daily at 10:00 A.M.; closing times vary. For information call (800) 63–SHAMU.

Just a few steps away from Sea World is **Geauga Lake.** After a busy year of schoolbooks and tests, your kids deserve to let loose during the summer at an old-fashioned amusement park. And a new Junior Admission price at just $5.95 for kids less than 48 inches tall makes the trip easier than ever on the family budget.

Once inside the park, your preschoolers will make a beeline for Butch

The whole family will enjoy the antics of Sea World of Ohio's playful sea lions. (Courtesy Sea World of Ohio)

Hightides Funtime Fortress, new in 1995 and designed by the Little Tykes Company. This castle-inspired ultra-jungle gym is every child's backyard dream come true. Older kids will head for the wilder times and the Texas Twister, where they'll spin over trees and do complete flips in midair at heights of more than 60 feet. Other roller coaster action includes the fearsome Raging Wolf Bobs, the curvaceous Double-Loop, the gravity-defying Corkscrew, and the classic Big Dipper.

Meanwhile, back on land, check out Turtle Beach, one of the park's most popular attractions. A liquid playground designed just for the junior set, it has all kinds of splishy-splashy, amphibious fun. Feel like Mom and Dad are being left out? There's also a water park for grown-ups, Boardwalk Shores, with three 70-foot-tall water slides, four serpentine wet slides, two water toboggans, and a huge wave pool. Who says kids have all the fun?

Get the whole gang back together for a ride on the popular Gold Rush log flume (just be prepared to get wet) or spin your way up fifteen stories and check out the park from the giant Skyscraper. When you need to rest your feet, relax with a ride around the park on the monorail, the hand-carved Illions carousel, or while you watch one of the many live musical shows.

The folks at Geauga Lake are so sure you'll have a good time that they've even established a "Funtime Guarantee" that allows you to return free if you don't enjoy yourself. The park is open May through September; hours vary during the season. Tickets are $17.95 regular admission (anyone more than 48 inches tall), $5.95 for junior admission. After 5:00 P.M., admission is $11.95 Monday through Friday. For more information call (216–562–7131) or write Geauga Lake at 1060 Aurora Road, Aurora, 44202.

PENINSULA

Seven million visitors each year can't be wrong. That's the number of travelers who head to the **Cuyahoga Valley National Recreation Area,** a 33,000-acre National Park area north of Akron. They come for the natural beauty, the miles of smooth Ohio and Erie Canal Towpath Trail to bike or hike, the many activities (including a lively folk music festival in June), and the **Cuyahoga Valley Line Railroad** passenger train, which makes a 52-mile trip through the scenic park with stops at Hale Farm and Village or downtown Akron.

All aboard! Your family will experience the clickety-clack of the tracks and the romance of the rails firsthand with a trip on the scenic railroad. From river floodplain and steep-cut valley walls to ancient stands of evergreen, you'll sit back and relax as the train journeys through historic sites and unspoiled natural areas. Grab a snack or a cool drink in the concession car, and pick up a memento for your favorite railroad buff at the onboard shop. Consider a fall-color train excursion, offered the month of October, for a ninety-minute feast for the eyes through some of the state's most beautiful scenery. Excursions, rates, and times vary; for more details contact the railroad at (800) 468–4070.

The national park is also home to a Visitors Center housed in a canalera building (now a canal history museum) that was once served as a home, a general store, a tavern, a hotel, and a dance hall. Canal lock demonstrations are conducted on weekends by park service staff and volunteers wearing period costumes.

The park is a pleasure year-round. Warm-weather visitors can opt to giddyap along the trails, explore rock ledges and caves, or swim in one of the many lakes. In winter, ice skating, cross-country skiing, sledding, or snowshoeing provide frosty fun. Downhill devotees head to the **Boston Mills Ski Resort** for wintry fun on seven slopes, six chair lifts, two surface tows, and **Brandywine Ski Resort,** with one triple, four quad lifts, three handle tows, and a vertical drop of 250 feet. For more information on either resort call (216) 657–2334. Waterfall enthusiasts have two to choose from: breathtaking Brandywine, and the smaller Blue Hen Falls, with a quiet woodland setting.

And there's more. For additional information on the park's many offerings stop at the Happy Days Visitors Center on Ohio 303, east of Peninsula. Rangers will provide you with information on things to see and do in the park. For a national park service brochure, contact 15610 Vaughn Road, Brecksville, 44141.

AMISH COUNTRY

Tired of faxes and the fast track? Pack up the gang, turn back the clock and escape to a simpler way of life, Ohio style. The pressures of modern life fade away quickly when visiting **Amish Country.**

Northeast Ohio is the home of the largest population of Amish in the world. About 35,000 of these "plain people" live in a settlement about an hour south of Cleveland that covers several counties—including Holmes, Wayne, Tuscarawas, and Stark. The gentle and deeply religious Amish culture shuns twentieth-century technology and comforts, choosing instead a more rural, simpler way of life. Things are made or grown by hand, resulting in craftsmanship that knows few comparisons.

There's plenty for families to see and do in this part of the state. For starters, take a ride on the **Ohio Central Railroad** in Sugarcreek. The one-hour train ride sputters along behind a steam locomotive at a leisurely 15 miles per hour and takes you through the north-central farmlands that are home to this peaceful people. If you're curious about the Amish way of life, take in the **Mennonite Information Center** near Berlin, which offers a video introduction to Amish Country, and the **Behald Cyclorama,** a 265-foot mural that traces Amish and Mennonite heritage back to the 1500s in Switzerland.

For a closer look at an Amish household, stop at **Yoder's Amish Home** in Walnut Creek. This now-unoccupied 116-acre working farm has two homes and a barn. The first home is typical of an Amish household in the late 1800s, with exposed wooden floors and simple furniture. The second is a more "modern" Amish home, with gas floor lamps and running water. The farm's buggy ride is a favorite of young visitors. A 220-seat restaurant was added in 1994.

As famous as the Amish are for their handcrafts, they're just as renowned for their food. Watch Alfred Guggisberg's famous Baby Swiss cheese being prepared—up to 2,500 wheels of cheese are made each day—in a Swiss-chalet-style building north of Charm. Don't forget to pick up some of the "holey" goods to take home. Across the road, enjoy old-fashioned Wiener schnitzel, bratwurst, and fresh-baked pies and cakes, while being serenaded by accordion players and yodelers at the **Chalet in the Valley Restaurant.**

Other places to get some wholesome vittles include the **Homestead** in Charm, with daily specials and a nationally recognized peanut butter pie, and **Der Dutchman of Walnut Creek,** the first Amish-style restaurant. It opened with just seventy-five seats in 1967 and now serves up to

3,500 meals on a busy day. Specialties include family-style dinners of preservative-free, pan-fried chicken, ham, and roast beef served with home-made bread. After eating, relax on the deck overlooking the valley or sit a spell on an old-fashioned rocker on the front porch.

And, in this part of Ohio, even fast food gets an Amish twist—the McDonalds in Millersburg has a drive-through window reserved just for buggies.

For more information on Amish Country, contact the Holmes County Chamber of Commerce (216–674–3975); Tuscarawas County Convention and Visitors Bureau (216–364–5453); Wayne County Visitors and Convention Bureau (216–264–1800); and the Berlin Area Visitors Bureau (216–893–3467).

BRUNSWICK

Autumn wouldn't be autumn without a visit to a U-pick farm and apple orchard. One of the best in the area is **Mapleside Farms** at 294 Pearl Road. This four-thousand-tree apple orchard surrounds a 300-seat restaurant, apple house, bakery, gift house, and ice cream parlor. For more information on the farm and its seasonal events call (216) 225–5576.

BATH

Are the Laura Ingalls Wilder books, including *Little House on the Prairie,* popular with your kids? If so, they won't want to miss **Hale Farm and Village,** located just north of Akron.

The smell of fresh bread baking draws visitors into the village. Once inside, families are treated to a rare view of life in Northeastern Ohio's early days. Here, the sound of the blacksmith's hammer hitting hot metal, the sight of a sawmill busily cutting wood, and the smell of hearty stew cooking over an open fire take you back to the days when, before sweeping up, you also had to make the broom.

Twenty-one buildings bring the mid-1800s to life. The farm and village are set in the time when Jonathan Hale and his family first arrived in the wilderness of the Western Reserve. Think life is hard in the twentieth century? Your kids will never complain about their chores again after learning about the workload shared by even the youngest family members of these brave early settlers.

Hale Farm is also the site of popular special events, including Family Day On The Farm, held annually in June; a Children's Day in July, where kids can participate in nineteenth-century games and chores, including whitewashing picket fences and running in a sack race; and Family Days in August. For a special treat, sign up for the "Breakfast With The Toymaker" or the "Hale Holiday Brunch" held in November and December. Other yearly activities include a rollicking Scottish fest, a popular Civil War encampment, and the autumn Hale Harvest Festival.

After a tour, stop in the well-stocked museum shop, where you'll find samples of handcrafted items made at the farm, including handblown glass, brooms, candles, and blacksmithing and woodworking items.

The farm is open from May through October. Hours are 10:00 A.M. to 5:00 P.M. Tuesday through Saturday; noon to 5:00 P.M. Sunday. Admission is $9.00 for adults, $7.50 for seniors, and $5.50 for children ages six to twelve. For more information call (800) 589–9703 or (216) 666–3711.

AKRON

Founded in 1825 and closely tied to the building of the Ohio Canal, Akron was once the center of a vast global rubber empire. Today the city remains best known as the corporate home to influential companies such as Goodyear and Uniroyal–Goodrich. The city is so closely identified with the beginnings and growth of the rubber industry that it has gained the nickname "Rubber City." A bit of Akron trivia: The original space suits worn by U.S. astronauts were made and fitted at B.F. Goodrich.

Despite its role as a technological leader, Akron respects its past, with plenty to keep history buffs of all ages busy. Here you'll find one of the most ornate residences in the state as well as one of the few hotels and shopping centers built in a former silo.

Ever sleep in a round room? You and your family will get the chance at the **Akron Hilton Inn,** part of the historic **Quaker Square** complex. The 196 rooms of the hotel are perfectly round and contain 450 square feet of space—50 percent more than the average hotel room. The rooms were converted from the massive Quaker Oats silos that once housed more than 1.5 million bushels of grain and are 120 feet tall and 24 feet in diameter.

Akron is known as the home of the breakfast cereal industry. It was here in 1854 that Ferdinand Schumacher began selling his homemade oatmeal, later founding Quaker Oats and becoming the undisputed "Oatmeal King of America." Not surprisingly, the once-white silos have been repainted "oatmeal," in honor of their beginnings.

Adjacent Quaker Square Mall and Entertainment Complex is one of the most unusual shopping centers in the country. Located in the heart of downtown Akron, it too was carved from the original 1800s Quaker Oats cereal mill. Today it houses thirty shops (kids love **My Little Red Wagon,** the **Quaker Train Shop,** and the oatmeal cookies at the **Mill St. Candy Co.,** all on the second floor) as well as restaurants and entertainment facilities. Tasty family fare is available at the popular **Depot Restaurant,** once the home of Akron's Railway Express Agency terminal. On weekends, you can enjoy pasta, pizza, and hobo chicken here surrounded by real railroad cars, locomotives, and one of the world's largest model train displays. Tiny train buffs are encouraged to climb on the great locomotive by the entrance. For hotel reservations, contact the Akron Hilton at (216) 253–5970.

The **Akron Civic Theatre,** with its opulent design and ceiling with blinking stars and floating clouds, is one of the few remaining "atmospheric" theaters left in the country. It was lavishly designed by Viennese architect John Eberson to resemble a night in a Moorish garden. A guided tour will remind kids of what people did for fun before the days of television. For more information call (216) 535–3179.

Quick quiz time: What did Thomas Edison, Alexander Graham Bell, and Johann Gutenberg invent?

Don't know the answers? Then run, don't walk, to **Inventure Place,** one of Akron's newest attractions. This dramatic contemporary building in downtown Akron pays homage to the great men and women who, through the ages, revolutionized the world with their inventions. It's a magical place where potatoes are clocks and eggs can fly. It's a place where you can pluck the sky or take off in a bathtub. It's a place where fun comes first and ideas come fast.

Also home to the National Inventors Hall of Fame, it pays homage to the spirit of scientific creativity. Colorful, hands-on exhibits, displays, and workshops are designed to help visitors appreciate how great thinkers have contributed to the American way of life and to inspire you and your children to appreciate, reward, and pursue creativity and invention.

More than 325,000 would-be inventors per year flock to this 77,000-square-foot facility, designed by internationally known architect James Stewart Polshek. It features 29,000 square feet of exhibit space and a wide variety of programs and activities. A special 20,000-square-foot exhibit and inventors workshop area lets you and your children be the inventors: Learn to animate your own cartoon using a computer or create your own laser show. You can also pilot a helicopter (inside the building, of course) and build your own sound system.

Afterward, wander along the building's centerpiece—the soaring, stainless steel sail that houses five tiers of National Inventors Hall of Fame exhibits featuring some of the nation's greatest inventors and their inventions. Although big names such as Edison, Ford, and Bell grab center stage, there are also tributes to lesser known but no less important inventors. Inventure Place is at 221 South Broadway; for information call (216) 762–4463.

One of the city's earliest inventors is honored at the **Stan Hywet Hall and Gardens.** If you're curious about how Ohio's "other half" lived, you'll find the answers at the state's largest private residence, once home to Frank A. Seiberling, cofounder of Akron's Goodyear Tire & Rubber. Built in 1915, the mansion is considered the finest example of Tudor Revival architecture in the United States.

For forty years the Seiberling family entertained community leaders and heads of state in this sixty-five-room home. Recalling an English country manor, the mansion features lush architectural features, richly carved paneling, molded plaster ceilings, and luminous stained-glass windows. It's surrounded by seventy acres of beautifully landscaped lawns and gardens, as well as a carriage house, greenhouse, and conservatory. Special events geared to families include the Decorated Egg Show held in April and the Christmas holidays, when the house is lavishly decorated inside and out. Admission is $6.00 for adults, $3.00 for children ages six to twelve. The hall, at 714 North Portage Path, is closed Mondays and major holidays. Call (216) 836–5533 for more information.

If the Stan Hywet house piqued your curiosity about rubber and its impact on Ohio history and economy, stop at the **Goodyear World Of Rubber** museum on Akron's east side to learn more about this revolutionary invention.

Wander through the exhibits on your own or take a guided tour tracing the fascinating discovery of this material many take for granted. The museum is on the fourth floor of Goodyear Hall, part of the company's headquarters complex on East Market Street. Admission is free.

Ever wonder how rubber is made? You'll learn as the museum traces the material's beginnings from Charles Goodyear's kitchen laboratory and follows the growth of the company founded in 1898 and named for him. The fascinating Charles Goodyear Memorial Collection traces the discovery of the vulcanization process that made rubber a practical material for many uses. The collection was exhibited for several years at the Smithsonian Institution before moving to Akron.

Other highlights include a simulated rubber plantation, Indianapolis 500 cars, an artificial heart, a history of blimps and other light aircraft, and exhibits that show how tires are made. The museum is open Monday through Friday from 8:30 A.M. to 4:30 P.M. Admission is free. For more information contact the museum at 1201 East Market Street or call (216) 796–7117.

When Columbus set foot in the Americas, he was greeted by animals and birds unlike any seen in Europe or Africa. This "New World" animal kingdom is the one featured at the **Akron Zoological Park,** located on Edgewood Avenue west of downtown.

Some zoos are overwhelming, offering more than a family can possibly squeeze into one day. Not so the Akron Zoo, which is manageable in an afternoon and perfect for preschoolers' short attention spans. The park features animals found in North and South America in a scenic, naturally wooded area.

Discover what the early explorers may have seen on their historic travels: bighorn sheep, bobcats, reptiles, jaguars, prairie dogs, porcupines, and the massive black bear. Many of these animals once roamed the areas that are now your backyard. Watch river otters cavort in a pool in an underwater viewing area; take a ride on a pony; feed cows, goats and other farm animals in the Ohio Farmyard; or learn about endangered species and what your family can do to aid in their preservation. The zoo is open 10:00 A.M.

to 5:00 P.M. Monday through Saturday, 10:00 A.M. to 6:00 P.M. Sunday and holidays, with additional evening hours in the summer. Special family events include Zoobilation, an annual birthday celebration, the Boo at the Zoo Halloween happening in October, and the annual holiday lights celebration in November and December. The zoo is open mid-April through mid-October. Admission is $4.00 for adults, $3.00 for seniors, $2.50 for children ages two to fourteen. The zoo is at 500 Edgewood Avenue; for information call (216) 434–9567.

Carousel Dinner Theatre is America's largest professional dinner theatre. Rising stars and established talents are featured in Broadway's best musicals. A popular spot for families, favorites have included *The Unsinkable Molly Brown, Nunsense II, The Will Rogers Follies,* and *Guys and Dolls.* The theatre is at 1275 East Waterloo Road; for reservations and an upcoming schedule call (800) 362–4100.

It's been called "The Greatest Amateur Racing Event In The World," but to the more than one million youngsters who have participated since the 1930s, it's just plain old-fashioned fun. One of Akron's most thrilling events to participate in or just watch is the annual **All-American Soap Box Derby,** which has been held at the city's Derby Downs each August since 1934. Local champs from all over the world (both boys and girls) ages nine through sixteen compete in gravity-propelled cars in a week-long celebration.

The idea grew out of the photographic assignment of Dayton, Ohio, newsman Myron Scott, who covered a race of boy-built cars in his home community. He was so impressed that he acquired a copyright for the idea and began development of a similar program on a national scale. The goals of the derby remain the same as they were when it was founded: to teach youngsters basic skills of workmanship, to foster the spirit of competition, and encourage the perseverance necessary to see a project through to completion.

The first All-American race was held in Dayton in 1934; it moved to Akron the next year for the central location and hilly terrain. Each year since (with the exception of World War II), youngsters from all over have made the pilgrimage to Akron with the racers they have built and driven to victory in their hometowns.

Three racing divisions keep the action lively: The stock division is for first-time builders; the kit car division is a more advanced model; the master's division features older entrants and encourages creativity and design skills. The week's festivities culminate in Race Day, when young drivers compete for scholarships and prizes. Hours and admission fees vary. For more information contact P.O. Box 7233, Akron, 44306 or call (216) 733–8723.

BARBERTON

It's ten degrees below zero. The weather outside is frightful, and your kids' mood is worse. Where can you take them for a little wonderful winter fun? Look beyond the usual ski slopes and toboggan runs to **Magic Waters,** Ohio's only indoor water park and one of just six in the country. It's located just south of downtown Akron.

Magic Waters brings you all the thrills and chills of a wet-and-wild endless summer all year long. Bring the suit and prepare to plunge down a giant three-story tube slide, journey along 200 feet of lazy river, get drenched under two waterfalls, explore a sunken submarine, or swim in the huge, 75-foot pool. Fitness buffs enjoy the therapy pool that is kept at a balmy eighty-eight degrees year-round. Winter? What winter?

Magic Waters is just minutes from I–76 at 457 Morgan Street. For more information call (216) 848–2400.

CANTON

One . . . two . . . three . . . hike! If football is your game of choice, rush over to the **Pro Football Hall of Fame** here for an insightful view of one of America's most popular sports. Canton was chosen as the hall's site because the National Football League was founded here in 1920.

Included in the modern four-building complex are four eye-catching exhibition areas, a football action movie theater, a research library, a snack bar, and a bustling museum store that sells licensed items from all of the NFL's twenty-eight teams. Twin enshrinement halls permanently honor the greats of pro football.

A 7-foot bronze statue of Jim Thorpe, the legendary hero of early-day pro football, greets visitors. Nearby, an Exhibition Rotunda tells the story of the sport's beginnings and includes priceless souvenirs and mementos of the early days. A 52-foot dome in the shape of—what else?—a football holds the Professional Football Today display, with representatives from each of the current NFL teams.

Also worth a gander is the art gallery, with winning, action-packed photos; the Leagues and Champions Room, where AFL and NFL histories are recounted and the Super Bowl series is chronicled in colorful detail; and the moving history of the Black Man in Pro Football, which honors early African-American players. The museum is also site of the weeklong Pro Football Hall of Fame Festival in July, in which football's greatest names meet in Canton for an exciting of array of activities that include a balloon classic invitation, food fest and fireworks, a ribs burn-off, drum corps competition, Kickoff Sunday, induction of the newest enshrinees and, of course, a rousing game at Fawcett Stadium.

Hours are 9:00 A.M. to 5:00 P.M. daily; 9:00 A.M. to 8:00 P.M. from Memorial Day through Labor Day. Admission is $7.00 for adults, $3.00 for children age six to fourteen. A better bet for large families: A special rate of $17 admits parents and all dependent children. The hall is at 2121 George Halas Drive N.W., Canton, 44708; for information call (216) 456–8207.

Canton is also home to the three-part **McKinley Complex,** including a National Memorial, a Museum of History and Industry, and Discover World. All honor President William McKinley, 1843–1901, originally from Canton.

The memorial is a double-domed structure, sheathed with pink granite from Massachusetts. Inside the memorial are the remains of the President and Mrs. McKinley, as well as their daughters Katie and Ida, who died in childhood of diphtheria.

Happier memories are found in the Museum of History, which recounts some 200 years of American history. Future homemakers imagine preparing a meal in the authentic pioneer kitchen; kids of all ages love the collection of historic toys spotlighting children's precious possessions before the days of Nintendo and television. Another section includes tangible remembrances of William McKinley: the clothing he wore, the furniture he used, personal and political mementos representing his life as a public and private figure. Other popular displays include the vintage "Street of Shops" and the operating HO gauge model train complex representing the Pennsylvania Railroad tracks through nearby Ohio towns such as Orrville, Massillon, Canton, Louisville, Alliance, and Sebring. Also located here are the Museum of Industry and a starstruck Planetarium.

Kids favor Discover World, an adjacent science center. From the minute you're greeted by the spine-tingling roar of a life-sized allosaurus (it moves its legs and opens its jaws thanks to the magic of robotics) at the entrance, you know you're not in another stuffy museum.

Wander inside and you'll find yourself in a landscape that reveals exciting secrets of many years ago. Explore the kinds of creatures that roamed the earth as you examine fossil remains and walk in the shadow of a massive mastodon's skeleton. Peek inside the circular tent of a long-vanished Indian tribe where dioramas show how Stark County prehistoric Indians might have lived. Farther along, you'll hear the trickle of water and the sound of birds as you pass through today's ecosystem and approach mankind's exploration of the next great frontier—outer space.

Once aboard Space Station Earth, you'll learn how lasers and light waves behave and the way air reacts under pressure. Pretend you're a meteorologist on TV and examine weather conditions in Ohio as well as around the world. Discover World encourages children to explore the past, present, and future.

The McKinley Complex is open Monday through Saturday 9:00 A.M. to 5:00 P.M. (until 7:00 P.M. during the summer) and noon to 5:00 P.M. on Sunday (until 7:00 P.M. during the summer). Admission is $5.00 for adults, $4.00 for seniors, $3.00 for children ages three to eighteen. The complex is located at 800 McKinley Monument Drive N.W. in Canton. For more information call (216) 455–7043.

BOLIVAR

Few think Ohio—a long way from the battlefields and cities of the East Coast—played a part in the American Revolution. The eighty-one-acre **Fort Laurens** here was the only American fort built in Ohio during the Revolutionary War. Today it's the home of many lively military reenactments and provides the kind of history lesson your children won't mind learning.

The fort traces the lives of the 176 men and 5 women who lived here more than two centuries ago. They had been sent to the Ohio country to neutralize the Indian threat and establish a western supply post for an eventual attack on British Detroit to the north. The fort was christened for

Henry Laurens, then president of the Continental Congress. After a long and bitter American occupation, the fort was abandoned in 1779 when hopes of attacking Detroit were given up.

A good overview of the site's history and an intriguing collection of artifacts found on archaeological digs can be found in the museum, which now sits on what was once the fort's west gate. Lifelike mannequins wearing uniforms of the period, weapons, and household goods help tell the fort's story, as does an informative, action-packed video.

Just outside the museum, the Tomb of the Unknown Patriot pays homage to the courage and perseverance of those who once lived at Fort Laurens and fought and died for American independence. A shallow trench surrounding a part of the museum outlines the shape of the original fort. Surrounding the museum is a large park—including a restful picnic area—where reenactments are held (it's also a great picnic spot). Hours for the museum and park vary. Fort Laurens is at Route 1, Box 442, County Road 102 in Bolivar; for information call (216) 874–2059.

Not far from the fort is another remnant of the state's past. **Zoar Village** was settled in 1817 by a group of pioneers seeking religious freedom. A group of 300 German Separatists—so named because they had broken with the established Lutheran church—left Germany and founded on the Ohio plains one of the most notable experiments in communal living in our country's history.

Life at Zoar, which means "a sanctuary from evil," was far from heavenly, however. Because food was scarce and work difficult to find, a communal style of living was adopted. Ahead of their time, the German Separatists believed in equality for men and women. The village grew and crops flourished, with a flour mill, planing mill, and woolen mill soon springing up. By the mid-1830s Zoar was self-sustaining, and the villagers had become known throughout the state for their skill in gardening.

Today, this quiet village offers a respite from the confusion of modern life. Many of the public buildings have been restored and welcome families curious about this bygone era.

First stop should be the former Zoar Store, built in 1833. Once the center of the community and the area's post office, it sold products produced in and outside the village. Today it's where you'll pick up your tour tickets and reproduction of nineteenth-century wares, as well as view an informative video on the village.

Don't miss the impressive two-story Georgian style **Number One House,** once the home of Zoar leader Joseph Baumeler. The home features fine examples of Zoar furniture and crafts. Not far away is the Garden and Greenhouse, built in 1835. The formal gardens throughout the village square were designed in a geometric plan based on the Bible; during their time, the villagers became known for their skill in gardening and design. Other popular stops include the 1825 Tinshop, the 1840 Wagon Shop, the 1834 Blacksmith Shop (with its great charcoal-fired forge and its huge bellows), and the 1841 dairy (the workers lived on the second floor). Finally, follow your nose to the 1845 Bakery, where Zoar members came once a day to receive, free of charge, as much bread as they needed. Today, demonstrations of the bakery's ovens turn out fragrant bread, pretzels, and gingerbread.

Zoar Village is at State Route 212 in Zoar and is open April through October; hours vary with the season. For more information call (216) 874–3011.

NEW PHILADELPHIA

In 1772, **Schoenbrunn Village** was settled by Moravian missionaries in an attempt to convert the local Delaware Indians to Christianity. It was here that the state's first schoolhouse was built to educate the Indian children. Despite its pacifist beliefs and its acceptance by the local population, Schoenbrunn was abandoned in 1777 because of the impending Revolutionary War and the advance of the British.

Today, the village has been restored to appear as it did more than 200 years ago. Costumed volunteers in eighteenth-century attire help bring history to life, recreating a fascinating and fateful time in Ohio history.

For a quick overview of the area, stop by the small museum near the village. Afterward, wander among the reconstructed buildings, which include a simple meetinghouse, the schoolhouse, a recently renovated visitor orientation center (which tells how the area's log cabins were made), and other buildings. Shoenbrunn Village is on East High Avenue in New Philadelphia; for information call (216) 339–3636. The village is open Memorial Day through Labor Day from 9:30 A.M. to 5:00 P.M. Monday through Saturday, noon to 5:00 P.M. Sunday; 9:30 A.M. to 5:00 P.M. Saturday and noon to 5:00 P.M. Sunday in September and October.

STEUBENVILLE

"Watch It Made in the U.S.A.," a new guide to companies that make America's favorite products, recently named Steubenville's colorful **Creegan Company** as one of the best factory tours in the country. It's worth the trip to this tiny town near the West Virginia border.

What makes Creegan so great? It's not so much the tour itself but what the company creates. Creegan is the nation's largest manufacturer of animated and costume characters. Familiar faces include Beary Bear, Plentiful Penguin, Strawberry Bunny, and the Gamuffins, who are seen in retail shops and malls across the country. Creegan also designs characters for Sea World, Hershey's Chocolate World, and Disney World.

Inside a former Montgomery Ward department store at the corner of Washington and Fifth Streets visitors of all ages watch as Creegan employees bring an array of characters to life. The three-floor factory bustles with activity as artists and craftspeople design, sculpt, decorate, and mechanize hundreds of animated creatures.

After being greeted by "Beary Bear," the company's official mascot, a costumed guide leads you through a room that contains what must be thousands of spools of ribbon in every color, pattern, and texture. Puppet heads, scenery, and props battle for space with silk flowers and other craft materials. A large, lifelike white gorilla stands beside three rosy-cheeked elves. Along the way, the tour, which lasts forty-five minutes to an hour, passes through the art, mechanical, carpentry, and sewing departments.

Up a wide staircase is the art shop, where workers make costumes and paint faces on molded plastic heads. On the main floor your kids will watch with fascination as a huge vacuum-form machine presses out the puppet faces and uses white plastic and molds to create various facial expressions.

Downstairs in the main sculpting area one woman creates all of the characters' head molds. Shelves contain hundreds of plaster molds shaped like heads, feet, hands, and animals. Farther along, in the mechanics/electronics department, brave children can peek inside some headless mechanized bodies to discover the characters' sophisticated electronic insides and see how the parts come together to produce body movements.

Tours are free and include cake, candy, or cookie samples from the company's Fancy Food Department. An on-site Christmas Shop features company-made items including trees, lights, ornaments, gifts, and decorations. New this year is the Grampa Creegan Puppet Shop, which displays hand and rod puppets and deluxe, plush, stuffed animals from around the world. Tours are offered Monday through Friday from 10:00 A.M. to 4:00 P.M., and Saturdays from 10:00 A.M. to 2:00 P.M.

The Creegan Company is at 520 Washington Street in Steubenville; for information call (614) 283–3708.

COSHOCTON

Derived from travelers' spellings of Indian words meaning either "river crossing" or "place of the black bear," this unusually named town on the banks of the Muskingum River was once called Tuscarawa. The legendary Johnny Appleseed planted some of his orchards here, but the town was best known as an important canal port and a thriving milling center from the 1830s through the Civil War. The town honors its heritage during the annual **Coshocton Canal Festival and Parade,** held each August to commemorate the arrival of the first canal boat, the *Monticello,* which docked in Port Roscoe in 1830.

A family favorite in town is **Roscoe Village,** named one of the twenty best historic restorations in America by *Early American Life* magazine. The original town fell on hard times after the canal closed in 1913, but it was reborn in 1968 as a living history museum, where interpreters and craftspeople bring the nineteenth century to life for thousands of happy visitors.

Start your visit with the wide-screen, multi-image show in the Visitors Center and then explore the village's seven living history buildings (including an early nineteenth-century house, a blacksmith shop, a schoolhouse, and an 1840s canal tollhouse) and nineteen unusual shops, or take the kids on a once-in-a-lifetime, forty-five-minute horse-drawn canal boat ride. Afterward, snack on goodies from the **Village Bakery,** sample regional cuisine at the 1838 Old Warehouse restaurant or cool off over homemade ice cream at **Captain Nye's Sweet Shop and Cafe.** Finally, bed down for the night amid Shaker-style furnishings in the fifty-one-room village inn. Many families prefer to visit during one of the annual events, including the rousing Dulcimer Days held each May. The festival features the mid-Eastern regional dulcimer championships as well as exhibits, sales, workshops, and performances on an open-air stage. Other popular weekends include Summer Fest, the Old Time Music Fest in September, Apple Butter Stirrin' in October, and the festive Christmas Candlelighting in December. Admission to the village is free; a tour of the historic museums is $6.00. Roscoe Village is at 381 Hill Street; for more information on special events or the village call (800) 877–1830; for reservations at the inn call (800) 237–7397.

LOUDONVILLE

Have your kids ever wanted to learn the right way to throw a tomahawk? If so, they'll have a field day during the **Great Mohican Indian Pow-Wow and Rendezvous** held twice yearly in Loudonville, in the southern part of the region. Here's their chance to see feather headdresses and war paint firsthand, as well as learn about the intricacies and long-standing traditions of Native American culture.

This is a real Native American pow-wow. Native Americans from tribes such as the Navajo, Cherokee, Lakota, Sioux, Shawnee, Seneca, Iroquois, Comanche, and Ottawa travel from around the country to meet on Mohican Valley territory for fellowship and competition.

Although the Traditional and Fancy Dance competitions are limited to Native Americans only, visitors are encouraged to enjoy the event as spectators. Tribes perform as their ancestors did for generations through movements that signify great spiritual meaning for Native Americans. The Pow-Wow offers non-Native Americans a rare chance to see this art form firsthand.

This multievent festival also includes Native American foods, storytelling, hoop dancers, herbalists, blacksmiths, and other demonstrations of Native American culture. Some thirty Native American craftsmen, including famous flute-maker and -player Arnold Richardson, will sell their wares, including potters, bead workers, silversmiths, quill workers, pipestone carvers, wood and bone carvers, leather workers, basket weavers, Indian painters, and musicians.

Admission is $6.00 for adults; $2.50 for children age six to twelve. Pow-Wows are held twice yearly, in July and September. For more information call (419) 994-3103.

MATERIALS PARK

Heavy metal. It's a strange sight rising from more than 45 acres of rolling hills. Has a spaceship set down right here in the farmland off Route 87 some 20 miles east of Cleveland, you wonder?

Nope. The huge geodesic dome, the largest open-face dome in the world, is the headquarters of **ASM International** and one of the most photographed sites in the state. Created by Cleveland architect John Terence Kelly, it was completed in 1959. One of the most outstanding features of the building is the dome, also known as a "space lattice" designed by R. Buckminster Fuller.

Defined by a network of hexagonal and pentagonal shapes, the openwork dome stands 103 feet high, 250 in diameter, and weighs some eighty tons. It's formed of 13 miles (65,000 parts!) of aluminum tubing and tension rods. In all, it resembles a giant, round honeycomb.

The huge dome has become a tourist attraction in itself, but visitors also enjoy the circular mineral garden set beneath the dome in a landscaped area. Educational as well as decorative, it displays more than seventy-five specimens of raw mineral ores, all labeled with identification for miniature rock hounds. A fountain sprays water 30 feet high in the center over the minerals below. A sundial on the other side of the garden accurately reflects the time of day.

Another favorite site is the apple tree grove. When Isaac Newton discovered the law of gravity, the Royal Society of England identified the apple tree he sat under and kept it. Before the tree died, cuttings were made. One ended up here in 1968. Originally marked and kept in a fenced-in area, it was later moved to a grove of similar-looking trees to protect it.

The building and grounds are open 8:30 A.M. to 10:00 P.M. daily. No organized tours are offered.

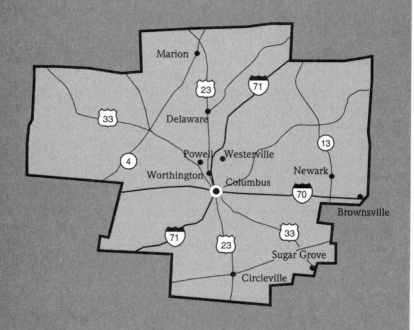

Marion

23   71

33

Delaware

13

Powell Westerville

Worthington Columbus Newark

70

Brownsville

71   23   33

Sugar Grove

Circleville

Central Ohio

CENTRAL OHIO

If Ohio is, as the slogans say, the "heart of it all," then Central Ohio is the "heart of the heart." The area is anchored by Columbus, the State Capitol, a bustling center of government, and the region's largest city. Beyond Columbus, however, are rolling farms and small towns that make this area one of the most picturesque in the state.

But Central Ohio is not all work and no play. Columbus is home to COSI, the "kid-tested and kid-approved" Center of Science and Industry, where you can ride a high-wire bicycle or step inside a lunar module. It's also home to the groundbreaking Wexner Center for the Arts, known for its mind-bending modern art exhibits. From city streets to country fields and everywhere in between, there's plenty to explore.

COLUMBUS

Ohio's capitol is reinventing itself. Once a sleepy governmental town, it's now a thriving city—the state's largest—on the cutting edge of scientific and technological progress. Local author and cartoonist James Thurber once said that "Columbus is a town in which almost anything is likely to happen and in which almost everything has." For families, that translates into an exciting city that knows how to have fun.

This is a city of firsts. The first banana split was made at Foeller's Drug Store in response to a customer request for "something different" and was originally called the "Five-Six-Seven." The first American kindergarten was established by German settlers in 1938. The first gorilla born in captivity made its debut in 1956 at the Columbus Zoo.

Downtown boasts a wide variety of things to see and do. For a waterside view of the city, consider a cruise on the *Crystal Lady.* This 45-foot glass-topped sightseeing boat, the city's first and the first privately operated vessel on the Scioto River since 1797, accommodates up to forty-nine passengers.

The boat cruises up and down the river, offering breathtaking views of the city skyline from the deck. As you cruise the Scioto on the forty-five-minute tour, you'll learn of the area's early Indian culture (the city was home to Adena, Wyandot, and Shawnee tribes) and hear about the early settlements (the city was once called Ohio City and Franklinton) and the historic development of the new town of Columbus. Besides the daily river tours, the *Crystal Lady* offers Music In The Air and Laser Light Concern cruises nightly, as well as special Moonlight Tours and lunchtime excursions. Tickets for the sightseeing cruises are $4.00 for adults, $3.50 for children, free under age two. For reservations and more information call (614) 224–1441.

The waterfront is also home to two of the city's most popular parks. **Bicentennial Park,** at Rich Street and Civic Center Drive, is the site of the explosive **Red, White & Boom** fireworks display held each July. The rest of the summer, it's a serene oasis in the city with beautifully landscaped grounds, a gurgling fountain, well-used bike trails, and the best skyline view in the city.

Battelle Riverfront Park, another great picnic spot, is also home to the flag-waving *Santa Maria,* a full-size, carefully crafted replica of Christopher Columbus's flagship. When he set sail in 1492, Columbus was carried by a 98-foot-long wooden ship called a *nao,* or typical merchant's cargo ship.

Five hundred years later, you can visit one of the world's most authentic representations of Columbus's flagship. Built for the city's 1992 Quincentennial celebration from ancient archives, the vintage vessel lets would-be sailors experience life on board a historic sailing vessel. Costumed interpreters tell how sailors of yore whiled away long days at sea, and tell stories of how they often ate cold meals due to fear of galley or kitchen fires. You'll also see their on-deck sleeping quarters. Staying in town for awhile? Consider booking a pirate-themed party for a birthday your child will long remember. The ship is open daily Tuesday through Sunday from April through December. For information contact 50 West Gay Street or call (614) 645–8760.

Back on land, a good place to get a feel for the pulse of the city—and the state—is the **Ohio Capitol Square Complex** on Broad Street. Who needs C-SPAN when you and your children can watch history in the making during a visit to one of the oldest statehouses in continuous use in the United States?

First used in 1857, it's affectionately called the "Hat Box Capitol" because of its distinctive rotunda and is considered one of the country's finest examples of Greek Revival architecture. Ironically, architect Frank Lloyd Wright considered it "the most honest of state capitols" even though much of it was built by penitentiary inmates. This majestic structure was built of Columbus limestone after the city became the state's third capitol in 1816. It's one of the few capitols around the country that doesn't sport a dome and is decorated with twenty-four-carat gold leaf. It took six architects twenty-two years to complete at a cost of $1,359,121.

After a quick introduction in the ground floor visitor's center, follow in the footsteps of Presidents Garfield and Harding, who both served in the Senate Chamber. Abraham Lincoln was speaking here in 1861 when he learned that the Electoral College had confirmed his presidential victory (the chair he sat in is still there). On a tour, you can see the Senate Building's 1901 Grand Staircase (don't forget to look up to see the state's seal depicted in stained glass in the skylight). Watch restoration workers in more than sixty rooms (the capitol's facelift is due to be completed sometime in 1996) or sit a spell in one of the many rooms while sessions are in progress and watch our government at work. You may find yourself concluding, as Ohio governor George Voinovich did, that "visiting the Statehouse is one of the best ways to educate young children and other visitors on what it means to be an Ohioan."

The capitol complex is open daily from 9:00 A.M. to 7:00 P.M.; guided forty-five-minute tours are offered Monday through Friday from 9:00 A.M. to 3:00 P.M.; on weekends, a tour guide is on site from 11:00 A.M. to 4:00 P.M. For more information call (614) 752–6350.

A bird's-eye view of the capitol complex is also available from the fortieth floor of the **James A. Rhodes State Office Tower Building** across from the rotunda. Tours of the Supreme Court are also given at the tower, located at 30 East Broad Street, Monday through Friday at 9:30 and 10:30 A.M. and 2:30 P.M. Reservations are required; call (614) 644–5250.

Across the street on Broad is another restored masterpiece, the Ohio Theater. The Loew's theater chain spent nearly $2 million to rebuild and redecorate what stands today as a premier example—one of the few remaining in the country—from the golden age of vaudeville and silent movies. The first sound movie, *The Tempest,* starring John Barrymore, was shown here in 1929.

The lavishly restored 2,897-seat theater is adorned with gold-plated trimmings and Tiffany chandeliers. Columbus residents raised funds to buy the beloved theater just minutes—literally, as the bulldozer was driving down the street—before the wrecking ball began demolition in the late 1960s. Since then, using volunteer labor, donations, and matching funds, the Ohio has been transformed into a lively theater of the performing arts, with a full schedule of events, including a popular summer classic movie series that draws families from all over Franklin County and beyond. The theater is also home to the Columbus Symphony Orchestra, BalletMet Columbus, and a Broadway comedy and musical series, making it the busiest performing arts facility in the state of Ohio. For a schedule and more information call (614) 469–0939.

Looking for a souvenir of your stay? Pick up anything your heart desires at the $200 million **Columbus City Center Mall,** adjacent to the Hyatt Hotel across from the capitol complex. Kids won't be able resist spending their allowance at the clever **Imaginarium** or the **Great Train Store,** which is overflowing with train memorabilia of all kinds by Lionel or Thomas the Tank Engine.

The downtown shopping center—one of the few in the country—has more than 150 shops for all budgets, including several of Columbus native and Limited founder Leslie H. Wexner's stores. There's also Marshall Field's, Jacobson's, and Ohio-based Lazarus as well as national restaurants and boutiques such as Gucci and Henri Bendel (the first location outside of Manhattan). The ever-tempting **A Show of Hands** gallery features the best of Ohio-made arts and crafts. The mall is at 111 South Third Street; for information call (614) 221–4900.

KHRISTI'S TOP FAMILY ADVENTURES IN CENTRAL OHIO

1. State Capitol Complex, Columbus
2. German Village, Columbus
3. Ohio Historical Society and Ohio Village, Columbus
4. Ohio State Fair, Columbus
5. Circleville Pumpkin Festival, Circleville

Just six blocks south of the State Capitol via Third Street is **German Village,** a friendly neighborhood that earned a spot on the National Register of Historic Places in 1975 because of the quaint brick homes set along its narrow cobblestoned streets. German immigrants settled the 230-acre area in the mid-1800s; it was narrowly saved from a freeway expansion and the wrecking ball in the 1950s. Curious about old-time Columbus? It's a great place to get an idea of how city residents lived in the nineteenth century.

Today it's home to young urban professionals and others who prize the area's heritage and historic charm. Chic coffeehouses sit side by side with quilt shops, neighborhood pubs, and authentic German bakeries.

Today's wanderers in German Village find well-tended cottages and stately mansions with flower-filled window boxes and wrought-iron gates. Daily tours are offered in the summer from the **German Village Meeting Haus** (588 South Third Street), where volunteers are also available to help design self-guided tours other times of the year.

Ideal for walking (but not always for parking), German Village is one of Columbus's major attractions, drawing more than 100,000 visitors a year. More than just a pretty piece of restored Americana, this is a working neighborhood, with businesses from supermarkets and dry cleaners to antique shops and bookstores. Strudel is still sold at **Juergen's Bakery and Restaurant** on South Fourth Street (614–224–6858) and bratwurst at **Schmidt's Sausage Haus,** on Kussuth Street, where they're also famous for their bet-you-can't-eat-it-all cream puffs (614–444–6808). **Thurn's,** on Third, is an old-fashioned and still popular lunch counter.

Another landmark is **Diebel's,** where the spicy sausage and sauerkraut are legendary and where even the kids get into the rollicking, good-time spirit during weekly polka parties and weekend sing-alongs. In the middle of it all is peaceful **Schiller Park,** twenty-three acres of greensward in the middle of the district's tree-lined streets and home to many of the area's bed-and-breakfast inns. Today this urban oasis has an amphitheater, tennis and basketball courts, a playground, jogging paths, and a recently restored lake. Pick up some sandwiches from nearby **Katzinger's Deli** (475 South Third), an area landmark voted "Best Deli in America" by *Bon Appetit* magazine, and dine *al fresco* at one of the park's shaded tables.

Take home a piece of German Village with a visit to the **Golden Hobby Shop** (630 South Third Street; 614–645–8329). Housed in a former school, it sells crafts made by senior citizens from the area, from wooden shelves and hard-to-find old-fashioned toys such as tops and hand-painted wooden airplanes to intricately pieced quilts and beautiful knits.

Avid readers of all ages can get lost in the nooks and crannies of the **Book Loft** (631 South Third Street; 614–464–1774; hours daily from 10:00 A.M. to 10:00 P.M.), where the store takes up an entire city block and where negotiating the twenty-five rooms of discounted paperbacks and hardcovers requires a map—and a limitless credit card. The selection of children's books and tapes is second to none. The quirky **Hausfrau Haven,** also on Third Street, has unusual greeting cards, soft drinks, fine wines, and a renowned homemade fudge. Mind the kids while you visit, however; playful signs warn that UNATTENDED CHILDREN WILL BE SOLD.

You might even see lederhosen on some natives during special events. The neighborhood is the spotlight of the annual **Haus und Garten Tour** the last Sunday in June as well as the **Candlelight Garten Tour** in August and a **Merry Christmas Tour of Homes**. It's also home to the city's wildly popular **Oktoberfest,** held ironically in early September. Adults can stamp along to oompah-pah music and sample local brews; the younger set can participate in an ice cream eating contest or the cream puff stuff, thrill to the free kiddie rides in the Kinderplatz, or enjoy family-style entertainment, including performances by Opera Columbus, the Columbus Junior Theater, and Grandparents Living Theater. It's *wunderbar!*

And if you're looking for a place to celebrate an older child's birthday, consider **Engine House No. 5,** known for its seafood. Located at 121 Thurman Avenue in German Village, it's housed in a restored firehouse and features servers sliding down a gleaming brass firepole, complete with celebratory cakes and sparklers. For information call (614) 443–4877.

For more information on German Village, contact the German Village Society, 588 South Third Street, Columbus, 43215 or call (614) 221–8888.

Had enough history? It's back to the future at the popular **Ohio Center of Science and Industry,** known affectionately as COSI, a short walk away on Broad Street. It's hard to tell who's having more fun here—the children or the so-called "adults." Dedicated to the conviction that science can be fun (you'll be convinced too after a visit), Ohio's only science center and one of only twenty-two such centers worldwide attracts more than 700,000 "kids" of all ages from all over the world each year and has served more than eleven million visitors since it opened in March of 1964.

Action-packed exhibits are spread out on three floors in a former 1906 Memorial Hall, now refitted with a modern solar front addition. Visit the outer reaches of the solar system in the Planetarium. Lift a car . . . all by yourself. Touch a 260 million-year-old concretion. Teach a computer to talk. COSI challenges you to explore, invent, imagine, probe, discover, and experiment at more than 1,000 interactive exhibits.

Where else can you climb aboard an authentic 1961 Mercury space capsule and prepare for launch, ride a high-wire bicycle to test the forces of gravity (there's also a protective net, of course), or pretend you're conducting laparoscopic surgery? Young explorers can also discover a dark simulated coal mine, complete with miners, equipment, and real coal; touch rats, turtles, baby chicks, and even—ugh—cockroaches in the AnimaLab; see how their great-great-grandparents lived in the Street of Yesteryear (kids love the 10,000-piece CrackerJack collection from the archives of Columbus's Borden Company and the old-fashioned Nickelodeon showing talkies featuring Betty

Boop and the Little Rascals); get a charge out of the Electrostatic Generator, or observe as Cyro the arc-welding robot shows off its amazing mobility on the Hi-Tech stage. Hands-on reaches new heights here.

Families congregate at the third-floor FAMILIESPACE, an area dedicated to helping families discover new things together. The whole gang gets into the fun at the new COSI clinic, a kid-size medical facility where you're the patient as children play doctor, ride in an ambulance, examine bones in an X ray, don lab coats, and even sew a few stitches. The adjacent KIDSPACE, decorated with bright tubes and colors, encourages little ones to try a wind xylophone, walk on a piano, type in a make-believe office, and even star in the their own newscast or rock video (a concession outside sells videotapes for $3.00 so you can record the performances for posterity).

Special events include Family Chemistry Days, Fantastic Fireworks (exploring the Science Behind the Boom), stimulating summer workshops, Camp-In overnight experiences, exciting traveling exhibitions, and more. Hours are Monday through Saturday 10:00 A.M. to 5:00 P.M.; noon to 5:30 P.M. Sundays. Family admission is $20; individual admission is $6.00 for adults, $5.00 for students ages thirteen to eighteen; $4.00 for children ages two to twelve. COSI is located at 280 Broad Street; for information call (614) 228–COSI.

After a fun-filled day at COSI, it's time to refuel. The first **Wendy's** restaurant, opened by R. David Thomas on November 15, 1969, is located across the street from COSI. Today there are more than 4,000 Wendy's Old Fashioned Hamburger restaurants worldwide, but few compare to the original, complete with the signature blue-and-white striped decor and pictures of the chain's red-haired, pig-tailed namesake. Indulge in a cool chocolatey Frosty or grab a burger and some fries before heading to your next stop.

After the excitement of COSI, you may want to wind down with a visit to the peaceful **Franklin Park Conservatory and Botanical Garden,** also on Broad Street. Located on twenty-eight acres within the lush eighty-eight-acre Franklin Park, the conservatory opened to the public in 1895. It underwent a dramatic change in 1992, when a $14 million expansion was built for AmeriFlora '92, a floral celebration marking Christopher Columbus's discovery of America.

This pleasing mix of glass and grace is home to approximately 10,000

Visit Ohio's Center of Science and Industry (COSI), *where the entire family can experience science firsthand.* (Courtesy Ohio Center of Science and Industry)

plants representing more than 1,200 species. They're displayed in six climatic zones, including the Himalayan Mountain Room, the Tropical Rain Forest, the Desert, the Pacific Island Water Garden, the Tree Fern Forest, and the Cloud Forest. Show your kids where coffee comes from; watch gardeners clip the delicate tiny trees in the Bonsai Garden or relax under the huge palms in the Palm House, also a popular spot for weddings. Young horticulturalists get a kick out of the Shaving Brush Tree, named because its flowers resemble old-fashioned shaving brushes. The conservatory is at 1777 East Broad Street; for information (614) 645–8733. Hours are 10:00 A.M. to 5:00 P.M. Tuesday through Sunday; Wednesday until 8:00 P.M. Admission is $4.00 for adults and $2.00 for children four to eleven.

Expansive Franklin Park is also home to the free **Kidspeak KidsFest,** which offers big fun for the small fry with an entire day dedicated to children each September. Presented by the city's Recreation and Parks Department, it offers performances, rides, hands-on activities, and family-oriented community-service information in a festive park setting.

Past years have included entertainment on four stages, roving performers, a children's maze, a miniature race car pit stop and obstacle course, and the ever-popular face painting. For information call (614) 645–3334.

Think Disney World does great things with shrubs? Forget mouse ears and simple elephants. Green thumbs of all ages also congregate at the downtown **Topiary Garden** on East Town Street. This fanciful landscape created by sculptor James T. Mason depicts pointillist painter Georges Seurat's *A Sunday Afternoon on the Island of La Grande Jatte* and includes fifty-two larger-than-life human figures, eight boats, three dogs, and a monkey. It's the only topiary garden in the country to include human figures. Watch gardeners snip and clip the figures into shape, and who knows what you'll be inspired to do with the bushes back home.

Miniature Monets won't want to miss the **Columbus Museum of Art,** closer to downtown on Broad Street. Ohio's first museum is known for its innovative traveling exhibitions and its small but excellent permanent collection (including the breathtaking $80 million Sirak Collection). The museum offers a relaxing respite from the city streets and a well-loved Impressionist collection. Bright abstractions such as Frank Stella's *Nasielsk III* or *La Vecchia Dell'Orto* (The Witch Of The Garden) and Deborah Butterfield's life-size horse of welded steel are family favorites and provide inspiration to young artists. Look too for works by two eminent Columbus artists—realist George Bellows and folk artist Elijah Pierce. The museum is worth a stop just for the well-stocked **Museum Shop,** which has a great children's corner with everything from Madeline books to make-your-own masterpiece kits. The museum is located at 480 East Broad Street; for information call (614) 221–4848.

Not far from the museum at 77 Jefferson Avenue is the **Thurber House,** one-time home to James Thurber, one of America's best loved humorists. Older kids and would-be writers and cartoonists are enchanted with this modest home where Thurber lived during his college days with his parents, two brothers, numerous pet dogs, and an occasional relative. Many of Thurber's best-known stories (available for sale in the small shop, once the dining room) are set here; it's here that the alarms sound at night, where the electricity leaks, and the bed has been known to fall unexpectedly.

This is no velvet-rope house museum, although artifacts and memorabilia from Thurber's long career fill the rooms. Today it's a lively writers' center and the popular site of summer "Literary Picnics" and winter "Evenings with Authors" series. The house is open daily from noon to 4:00 P.M. for free, self-guided tours. For more information contact (614) 464–1032.

Columbus is a town that prides itself on its strong support of the arts. One of the best places in the city to see cutting-edge visual arts is the 250,000-square-foot **Wexner Center for the Arts.** Located near the heart of the Ohio State University (OSU) campus and dedicated to vanguard artistic activity, it opened in 1989 and was designed to be "an architectural event" and a center for the presentation and study of contemporary arts.

With a multidisciplinary approach including exhibitions, media arts, performing arts, and education, the center encourages continuous exploration and research in the arts. The four galleries host traveling exhibitions from modern art museums around the world, including the Museum of Modern Art in New York, the Walker Art Center in Minneapolis, and the Centre Georges Pompidou in Paris, as well as a popular avant-garde film series. The center is located at North High Street and Fifteenth Avenue on the OSU campus; for more information and current hours call (614) 292–0330.

Speaking of the Buckeyes, don't leave Columbus without a stop at **Ohio State University,** one of the largest universities in the country. A free, two-hour tour that departs from Drake Union includes the residence hall, the main libraries, and the famous football stadium—home to a long tradition of gridiron glory. A little-known fact: The campus was designed by Frederick Law Olmsted, who designed New York's famous Central Park in the 1880s. Tours depart from 1849 Cannon Drive; for more information call (614) 292–3980.

Ohio State football is big business in Columbus and across the state. Buckeyes from all over the country make pilgrimages to the campus, which is the site of tailgate parties and intense rivalry on crisp autumn weekends. But there's also lots of other sports action in town. Although invitations from the major leagues haven't piled up at Columbus' door, city

TOP ANNUAL EVENTS
IN CENTRAL OHIO

Red, White, & Boom!, July, Columbus; (614) 263–4444
Ohio State Fair, August, Columbus; (614) 644–3247
German Village Oktoberfest, September, Columbus;
   (614) 221–8888
Italian Festival, September, Columbus; (614) 294–5319
Circleville Pumpkin Festival, October, Circleville;
   (614) 474–7000
Columbus International Festival, November, Columbus;
   (614) 228–4010

residents take pride in their AAA baseball club, the **Columbus Clippers,** a farm team for the New York Yankees. They play at the 15,000-seat Clipper Stadium, not far from downtown, from May through October.

The Clipper Stadium is the site of popular birthday parties where, for just $7.50 per person, guests receive a reserved seat, hot dog, and refreshments and the birthday boy or girl gets his or her name on the scoreboard, free personalized baseball card, and a visit from the team's mascot, Captain Clipper. Regular special events include "Kids' Club Night" every Monday, with free general admission for children twelve and younger, and "Fireworks Night," with a spectacular fireworks extravaganza following Friday games. "Family Day at the Ball Park" is one of the best deals around, when the whole family (two adults and up to four children eighteen and younger) is admitted for just $8.00. Call (614) 462–5250 for tickets and schedules.

As home to the state capitol, Columbus is the appropriate home of the **Ohio State Fair.** If your kids think milk comes from a plastic carton, it's time to check out this annual event held every year in August since 1848.

Grab your "fair" share of fun as the state goes "whole hog" with a cornucopia of fun-filled activities and Ohio-grown riches overflow at the Ohio State Fairgrounds, not far from downtown Columbus.

The chance to bring home the blue ribbon brings out the best the state has to offer in livestock, agriculture, horticulture, and the creative arts. And there's always the exciting chance to see things like the largest pumpkin or taste award-winning homemade apple pie and stick-to-the-roof-of-your-mouth cotton candy, a fair staple.

City kids will love watching the grooming in the livestock area, where more than 20,000 spanking-clean farm animals are exhibited, or the hilarious racing pigs contest. Horse lovers head for the nation's largest All-Breed Horse Show, featuring more than twenty-seven breeds. Other exciting attractions include a championship rodeo; truck and tractor pulls; Hollywood stunt shows; motorcross races; a classic midway filled with awe-inspiring rides, games, and food concessions; and petting zoo and a free Kiddie Park. Grab a corn dog, buy a wristband that entitles you to ride all day long, and the day is yours.

Other family fun highlights include the dazzling Laser Light Adventure, performed free outside the coliseum nightly, the Olde Tyme Big Top Circus, Barn Tours, and the free Petting Zoo. At night, wind down with free entertainment at **Celeste Center,** featuring some of the greatest names in the business. Hundreds of free performances will have you singing along and tapping your feet. And if you're feeling really adventurous, check out the Ejection Seat, which shoots volunteers fourteen stories into the air in just three seconds.

For a great deal, head for the fair on one of the annual Family Value Days, when kids younger than age twelve are admitted free and parents pay the $3.00 children's fee. Regular prices are $6.00 for adults, $3.00 for children age five to twelve, with children free under age five. A ride-all-day wristband is $11.00. For schedules and more information call (800) BUCKEYE. The cavernous state fairgrounds are also the winter home of the **Columbus Chill Hockey Team,** which takes to the ice November through March. For tickets and more information call (614) 791–9999.

Across from the fairgrounds off I–71 you'll also find the **Ohio Historical Center and Ohio Village.** Who needs a time machine when you can travel from the Ice Age to the Space Age in just a few hours? Step back in time with a visit to the center's extensive collection and its adjacent re-created Civil War–era village.

The center, housed in a distinctive modern-looking building visible from I–71, packs a million years of history into 250,000 square feet of space. Permanent exhibits and varied displays examine the area's prehistory, history, and natural history. Meet the state's oldest inhabitants in "The First Ohioans" display with materials from the state's prehistoric cultures. Because of this exhibit, the *Smithsonian Guide To Historic America* named the center "the finest museum in America devoted to pre-European history."

Other fascinating displays include *Ohio: Two Centuries of Change,* which explores the state from 1770 to 1970, encompassing early settlement to the Civil Rights era. Here you'll find everything from a re-creation of a mid-nineteenth-century carriage company (complete with huge pulleys) and a 1907 fire engine to a working millstone and a jazzy 1957 jukebox that once graced an Ohio diner.

"The Nature of Ohio," the center's newest exhibit, has drawn rave reviews from families. The exhibit's entrance is guarded by a huge Conway Mastodon. A favorite with generations of children, the 10,000-year-old elephantlike skeleton was found in 1894 beneath four feet of swampy ground in Clark County, Ohio, and has tusks that measure 9½ feet long. Kids also congregate by the two-headed calf from 1910, the 1926 Egyptian mummy, and the rock and mineral displays.

Another popular exhibit traces animals native to the state—including the huge bison, once abundant in Ohio, which vanished during early settlement—that are now extinct. Stop by the well-stocked gift shop on the way out and peruse the many Ohio-related items, including Civil War caps, city puzzles, and Indian mound replicas. Don't leave without letting the kids taste one of the nine flavors of rock candy for sale. This old-fashioned treat still satisfies modern sweet tooths.

When you're tired of being inside, head down the gravel path to Ohio Village. Featuring costumed interpreters, talented artisans selling handmade period-style goods, and a rustic 1860s restaurant, it's a charming and educational trip back in time.

This a real working village. Students outside the one-room school-

Step back in time with a visit to Ohio Village, a re-created Civil War–era village with costumed interpreters and artisans who sell period-style goods. (Courtesy Ohio Historical Center)

house from 1855 swill root beer and play nineteenth-century games. Chat with "shopkeepers" and "townspeople" as they go about the tasks of pre-Civil War daily life.

There's also a Town Hall, which features a collection of Civil War artifacts; a print shop, where an award-winning printer still produces broadsides with original hand-cut woodblocks using antique presses; a general store, which sells reproductions of 1860s goods, including a tasty black licorice (it also includes a post office where you can have your postcards stamped with the official Ohio Village postmark); an inn and hotel (which now serves meals and refreshments) as well as a number of offices and shops.

In order to give an accurate depiction of nineteenth-century life, the village also includes some less pleasant aspects of the time: Roads are unpaved and dusty; there's even an undertaker's shop. On weekends, the Ohio Village Singers and other musicians add a festive note. The village and center is at 1982 Velma Avenue; call (614) 297–2300 for information. Hours vary depending on season.

A little farther east is Port Columbus International Airport, home to the **Ohio History of Flight Museum.** Aviators of all ages flock to the state's only general and commercial museum of its kind, featuring vintage antique aircraft made in Ohio, propellers, engines, and exhibits on the early days of aviation. There is also personal memorabilia from famous Ohio aviators. Open Monday through Friday 9:00 A.M. to 4:00 P.M. Saturday noon to 4:00 P.M., Sunday 1:00 to 4:00 P.M., admission is $2.00 for adults, $1.50 for kids. The museum is at 4275 Sawyer Road; call (614) 548–7917.

Willie Wonka fans might want to head west on I–270, where, not far from downtown, they'll find the **Anthony–Thomas Candy Company.** This longtime city institution and one of the largest family-owned candy-making facilities in the United States has been making chocolate in Columbus since 1916 and recently moved into a new, 152,000-square-foot factory.

You'll be licking your lips while you tour the new facility. In about an hour tour guides explain the candy-making process from start to finish. You'll watch workers create candy fillings in huge copper kettles as you walk along the comfortable, glass-enclosed overhead passageway. Guides point out several production lines (eventually, eight lines will produce 60,000 pounds of chocolate daily) as well as the unusual silver pipes that carry liquid chocolate through the factory. The tour ends in the 2,500-square-foot retail store (there are also fifteen retail stores in the Columbus area). Tours are offered by appointment from 9:00 A.M. to 3:30 P.M. weekdays. The factory is at 1777 Arlingate Lane in Columbus. To schedule a tour call the Candy Factory Hotline at (614) 274–8405.

This Bud's for You. While you can't taste the spoils on the **Anheuser–Busch Brewery Tour,** your kids will be amazed by the huge, four-story fermentation tanks and other facets of the free, hour-long tour. Just off I–71 in Columbus, families watch as barley malt, rice or corn, hops, yeast, and water are made into one of the world's best-selling beers.

After an introduction in the Welcome Center, you'll learn all about the Busch process, which includes rare beechwood aging. You'll follow a tour guide to the viewing area overlooking the Brew Hall, where natural ingredients are added to mashing tanks and brew kettles. You'll learn how the natural brewing process takes more than thirty days, with careful attention given to each step, and see displays tracing the history of the company and the beer industry. At the end, you'll see the newest addition—giant fermentation tanks four stories tall—and have the chance to sample brews in the hospitality room or browse in the gift shop. Tours are offered year-round from 9:00 A.M. to 4:00 P.M. Monday through Saturday. Anheuser–Busch is located at 700 East Schrock Road in Columbus; for information call (614) 847–6465.

POWELL

When the **Columbus Zoo,** located northwest of the city in Powell, was established in 1927, it cost 10 cents to enter. Today, admission is slightly more, but you still get a lot of fun for your buck.

Like many of its large and powerful animals, the zoo was tiny at birth. It was established in 1927 to house a small collection of donated animals. From this humble beginnings it has developed into one of the fastest growing and most highly acclaimed zoos in the nation.

It's had plenty of firsts. In 1956 the Zoo made headlines with the birth of Colo, the first gorilla born in captivity. Since then, generations of other lowland gorillas have been born here. The zoo also won international recognition for its breeding programs and its protection of many rare and endangered species. It's also known for its former director, Jack Hanna, who was seen for years cavorting with Johnny Carson and a parade of animal guests on "The Tonight Show."

Today, the zoo is home to more than 700 species and 11,000 specimens spread out on rolling, well-manicured grounds. While you'll find plenty of the "regulars" such as lions, tigers, and bears, it's also one of only four U.S. zoos to exhibit bonobos, also know as pygmy chimpanzees. And it's one of the few zoos in the nation to permanently exhibit koalas, which are featured in an Australian exhibit that also has wallabies, emus, and black swans.

Pint-sized animal lovers won't want to miss riding on the bumpy back of an Asian camel (the less adventurous can also take pony rides in the Kids Zoo), paddling about the Scioto River on the zoo's sternwheeler or exploring the indoor Discovery Reef, with more than 400 colorful species—including stingrays and sharks—in huge tanks, and a special tidepool where curious kids can touch starfish, sea urchins, and other aquatic creatures. Head for the playscape when your miniature safarians need to blow off a little steam; it has ropes and playscapes for climbing, a wooden ship to man, and more.

New in 1995 is the Flamingo/Alligator Display housing animals native to the southern United States and the Caribbean; an area featuring species native to the Ohio Wetlands; and a display that dispels myths about sharks (with a shallow tank where kids can even touch an 18-inch shark). Popular seasonal events include Boo At The Zoo in October and the Wildlight Wonderland, when more than 750,000 twinkling lights, displays, and rides for children welcome the holidays. The zoo is located at 9990 Riverside Drive, Powell, 43035, and is open 365 days per year from 9:00 A.M. to 6:00 P.M. Memorial Day through Labor Day and 9:00 A.M. to 5:00 P.M. the rest of the year. Admission is $5.00 for adults, $3.00 for children ages two to eleven, and free for children under two. For more information call (614) 645–3400.

Does watching sea lions and penguins cavort make your budding zoologists wish for some wet-and-wild adventures of their own? Luckily, the zoo is adjacent to the eighteen-acre **Wyandot Lake Waterpark,** which offers "good clean fun" from May through September. Grab the suits, the sunscreen, and the camera (just make sure it's waterproof) and catch a wave.

Nothing quenches a thirst for fun like a day at Wyandot Lake, where you can take the sizzle out of summer. Get drenched by a burst of tropical showers and unpredictable geysers as you weave through Zuma Falls' twisting turns and whitewater rapids. Blast through the slippery dark as you speed down six stories of tunnels in less than thirty seconds on the twisting and turning JetStream ride. When you need a relaxing break, kick back, grab an inner tube, and enjoy a lazy float down 850-foot-long Canoochee Creek or challenge the ocean surf of the Wild Tide's million-gallon wave pool. With more than sixty great rides and attractions, Wyandot Lake is among Ohio's best waterparks.

Little ones get into the watery action with a swim in the Tadpool or while exploring Buccaneer Bay, a multicolor, multiactivity water playground with geysers and gizmos built just for kids. There are even offerings for landlubbers, including eighteen classic dry rides that include a wooden roller coaster, an authentic antique 1914 carousel, a Kiddieland full of miniature boat and car rides, minigolf, go-carts, live entertainment, and more.

Having too good a time to go home? Dive-In Movie Nights let guests enjoy comedy and adventure films while floating and splashing in the wave pool or lounging on the shores of Parrot Cove. You'll never prefer the home VCR again.

Hours vary with the season. Prices are $13.95 for adults, $11.95 for kids 42 inches and shorter. For more information call (614) 889–9283.

DELAWARE

Not far north of Columbus via U.S. 23 and I–270 are the **Olentangy Indian Caverns.** For a better understanding of the people who settled this part of the country a visit here is a must.

Formed millions of years ago by an underground river cutting through solid limestone, today the caverns are a maze of winding passages and spacious underground rooms. There is evidence that the Wyandot Indians used the caverns as a haven from the weather and their enemies. One of the larger rooms contains the Council Rock, believed to be used for tribal ceremonies. The caverns were discovered by J. M. Adams, whose oxen broke lose from his wagon train in 1821 and were later found dead at the bottom of the cavern's entrance. Adams's name and the date of his discovery can be seen on the wall to this day.

Miniature explorers love descending the concrete stairs 55 feet into the cool, three-level caverns or touring the cavehouse museum that houses Indian artifacts and geological displays. Let them spend their allowance in the Indian-themed gift shop and afterward enjoy a picnic lunch, explore adjacent **Frontier Land** (have your name printed on a Wanted poster in the print shop) or relax with a round of minigolf while the kids hit the playground. Open daily 9:30 A.M. to 5:00 P.M. April through October, the caverns are located at 1779 Home Road, Delaware, 43015; for information call (614) 584–7917.

WORTHINGTON

The new Rock 'n' Roll Hall of Fame may be in Cleveland, but plenty of memories shake, rattle, and roll at **Dick Clark's American Bandstand Grill** in this Columbus suburb. Open less than two years, it sports vintage photos, gold and platinum albums, rare posters, artists' contracts, and more on the walls and tabletops. It's all from Clark's personal collection.

You'll also see classic "American Bandstand" footage from the original TV series on screens throughout the restaurant. Cuisine is all-American and reflects regional fare from across the country: New Orleans jambalaya, Santa Fe chicken fajitas, Philly cheesesteaks, or a classic burger and fries. And not all of the memorabilia is from the 1950s—your kids will recognize photos of Mariah Carey and other current superstars mixed in with the luminaries of yesteryear.

The grill is at 100 Hutchinson Avenue, just off I–270 and High Street. It's open for lunch and dinner daily. For more information call (614) 785–1985.

MARION

What little boy—and more and more, little girls—haven't grown up wanting to be president? Ohio has given the country many presidents, including Warren G. Harding, a Marion native and the country's twenty-ninth president. During the 1920 presidential campaign, he addressed voters from the wide front porch of his 1891 Victorian-style boyhood home. It later became known as his "front-porch" campaign.

Indulge your would-be statesmen and stateswomen with a visit to this impressive presidential home and museum. Today, your family can take a guided tour of the **Harding Home,** which has been meticulously restored and holds authentic furniture, statues, and clothing used by Warren and his wife Florence Harding from 1891 to 1920. Check out the original gaslights and the press building at the rear of the house, now a museum that displays memorabilia including the podium used at Harding's inauguration in 1920. The nearby Harding Memorial, located south of

Marion on State Route 423 and set in a peaceful ten-acre landscaped park, was built from public donations, including dime contributions from state schoolchildren. The house is at 380 Mt. Vernon Avenue. For hours and other information call (614) 387–9630.

But Marion isn't all about presidents and politics—it's also about popcorn. The zany **Wyandot Popcorn Museum** features a three-ring circus tent full of old-fashioned fun with a priceless collection of antique popcorn poppers, peanut roasters, concession trucks, and vintage popcorn wagons dating between 1890 and 1940. George Brown, a museum board member and former chairman of the board of the Marion-based Wyandot Company, maker of popcorn snacks, was instrumental in putting the collection together. Today it's the only one of its type in the world.

Rare models include the 1915 Holcomb & Hoke, the earliest automated popper, and the 1927 Cretors Eclipse, the first all-electric popper. There are forty-eight other vintage and restored popcorn machines in the former U.S. post office. You can also see demonstrations of ten steam engines, two of which are spring driven. The museum is located at 169 East Church Street and is open 1:00 to 4:00 P.M. Wednesday through Sunday through October, November through April just weekends. For more information call (614) 387–4255.

Visitors to the **Charlie Sens Antique Auto Museum** off U.S. 23 in Marion are greeted with the melodies of an old-fashioned calliope and the sight of a fully restored 1946 Piper Cub suspended from the ceiling at the main entrance. From a 1903 Ford, one of only twenty remaining in the world today, to a 1969 Corvair sporting just 11 miles, the museum traces America's automotive beginnings and has more than 100 of the world's most beautiful cars on display.

All the cars are in perfect running order and look as if they could be driven from the museum floor for a Sunday ride. The museum is the result of the passion of Ohio businessman Charlie Sens, a longtime collector who decided as his collection grew to open this sporty museum. Hours are 10:00 A.M. to 5:00 P.M. Monday through Saturday, noon to 5:00 P.M. Sunday. Admission is $5.00 for adults, $3.00 for students. The museum is at the junction of State Route 95 and U.S. 23. For more information call (614) 389–4686.

What would fall be without a visit to a U-pick farm? **Lawrence Orchards** in Marion has been serving families since 1921. This family-run orchard and farm market has a lock on home-grown freshness and is the location for the popular Orchard Harvest Craft Fair in August and the rollicking Applefest in September. The Orchards are at 2634 Smeltzer Road; for information call (614) 389–3019.

WESTERVILLE

You don't have to be a motorcycle mama or sport a black leather jacket to enjoy a visit to the tasteful **Motorcycle Heritage Museum,** located east of Olentangy Caverns on I–270. With more than sixty bikes dating from the late nineteenth century to the present, the museum traces the technology and design of motorcycles and celebrates the personal accomplishments and historic milestones that have given the sport its own special allure.

The museum opened in 1990. On permanent display is a replica of the 1885 wooden Daimler motorcycle, a 1912 Henderson, a streamlined 1941 Harley Davidson WL, an orange and black iron-barreled XR750 Harley and more. Even if you have never ridden a "hog," you'll laugh at some of the early designs and marvel at the range of invention and intricate technology that has made this mode of transportation one of America's most enduring. An on-site gift shop lets you go "whole hog" on motorcycle memorabilia.

The museum is at 33 Collegeview Road; for information call (614) 882–2782. Hours are 8:30 A.M. to 5:00 P.M. Monday through Friday, 10:00 to 4:00 P.M. Saturday; noon to 4:00 P.M. Sunday. Admission is by donation.

CIRCLEVILLE

Everyone knows that the Pilgrims ate pumpkin pie at their second Thanksgiving dinner. Yet even before that settlers were making pumpkin stew and pumpkin soup, even drinking pumpkin beer. The world's largest festival honoring this Halloween trademark began as a small exhibit in 1903 of pumpkins and corn fodder in this town 25 miles south of

Columbus. Today it has grown into a four-day extravaganza of parades and contests known as the **Circleville Pumpkin Festival.**

For several days each October the Pumpkin Festival bills itself as "The Greatest Free Show On Earth." The festival lures of hundreds of thousands of "pumpkin people" with displays of giant pumpkins (some as large as 400 lbs.!) and the world's largest pumpkin pie (one year it weighed 350 lbs. and was 5 feet in diameter). Kids get into the fun with contests for the best pumpkin poster and decorations—carved and painted pumpkin heads, funny facial expressions, strangest hat.

Ever tasted pumpkin fudge or pumpkin burgers? How 'bout french-fried pumpkin chips? You can here. There are also booths selling pumpkin delicacies, agricultural exhibits, clowns, bands, rides, games, and even a huge "pumpkin tree" in the center of town. For more information contact the Pickaway County Visitors Bureau (614–474–4923).

NEWARK

Do your kids like solving mysteries? Give them a crack at the **Newark Earthworks,** part of what once was the most extensive earthworks in the country. These geometric enclosures were believed to have been used by the Hopewell Indians (1000 B.C.–A.D. 300) for social, religious, and burial ceremonies but their real purpose remains shrouded in mystery. The Hopewell people lived primarily in Central and Southern Ohio along the major river valleys such as the Miami, the Scioto, and the Muskingum. Yet despite a strong family structure and a complex way of life, the culture disappeared around A.D. 500–600.

The earthworks are fascinating to explore. The Hopewell's engineering feat is preserved in Wright, Octagon, and Moundbuilders earthworks and **Moundbuilders Ohio Indian Art Museum,** the nation's first museum devoted to prehistoric Native American art.

Archaeologists have found pipes and some ceremonial objects at the sites. Necklaces and bracelets were common ornaments, with beads made from pearls or cut from freshwater or marine shells. A number of small figurines excavated from several Hopewell sites show that the women wore knee-length skirts and moccasins; men wore breechcloths, belts, and moccasins. Both wore garments made of skins and used feathers for headdresses.

The Newark earthworks cover an area of more than 2 miles. Although the expansion of the city has obliterated parts of the walls and many of the mounds, important sections are preserved in Octagon State Memorial, with 138 acres, and in Moundbuilders State Memorial, with 66.

Within the fifty-acre Octagon Earthworks are small mounds. The Great Circle Earthworks, with conjoined mounds in its center, is located in the Moundbuilders State Memorial. This embankment is approximately 1,200 feet in diameter with earthen walls ranging from 8 to 14 feet high. Approximately ¼ mile northeast are the Wright Earthworks, a small section of a large enclosure that was once part of the original Newark works.

For a better understanding of the Hopewell culture and the fascinating people who built these earthworks, stop at the Ohio Indian Art Museum. The first museum devoted exclusively to Native American art was opened in 1971 at Moundbuilders State Memorial. Objects inside represent the artistic achievements of all known prehistoric cultures in Ohio from 10,000 B.C. to A.D. 1600. For information call (800) BUCKEYE.

BROWNSVILLE

After touring the Newark earthworks, visit **Flint Ridge State Memorial** not far away. Many centuries ago Indian trails from villages and campsites throughout the Midwest converged on this irregular range of hills about 10 miles in length, located between the modern cities of Newark and Zanesville. Prehistoric Indians made their way to these hills for a material key to their survival—flint. Today, this semiprecious stone is also the official gem of the state of Ohio.

Nowhere in the Midwest has better flint been found than this area. Eventually, quarry operations were established to extract the highly prized semiprecious stone. Large hammerstones weighing up to twenty-five pounds were used to wedge natural cracks into the rock.

In 1933 the Ohio Historical Society established the 525-acre memorial to preserve this unusual site. In 1968 a modern museum was founded over one of the original pits. Here would-be geologists and historians learn about the industrial and human history of this unusual area and visit displays that show the types and location of flint deposits in Ohio, how flint was formed, and modern objects made of this natural resource.

Afterward wander along the asphalt trails that cut through the memorial's nature preserve and wildlife trails. The preserve was created by flint pits that filled up with water and formed temporary ponds and homes for wildlife and plants. For more information on Flint Ridge call the Ohio Historical Society at (614) 297–2332.

SUGAR GROVE

In 1931 Dr. Frank Warner of Columbus gave his bride Carmen a peculiar wedding gift: ninety-four acres of old farmland in southern Fairfield County. Mrs. Warner named her estate **Wahkeena,** an Indian word meaning "most beautiful," after a waterfall she had seen in Oregon.

In 1957 Mrs. Warner bequeathed Wahkeena to the Ohio Historical Society "to be used for nature study and as a preserve for birds and other wildlife." Today, the 150-acre Wahkeena serves as an outdoor classroom for thousands of the state's young novice naturalists and budding bird-watchers. A log lodge, large pond, and rock formations sculpted from ancient sandstone add to the preserve's calm beauty.

The site regularly hosts hikes, classes, and seminars. Visitors may browse in the nature center or stroll the serene trails, identifying ferns, trees, and wildflowers with the aid of the site's series of nature guides. Hours are 8:00 A.M. to 4:30 P.M. Wednesday through Sunday from April through October and by appointment Monday through Friday from November to March. The preserve is at 2200 Pump Station Road; for information call (614) 746–8695.

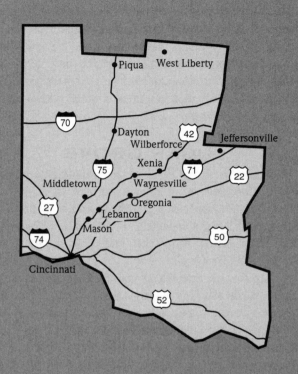

Piqua
West Liberty
70
Dayton
42
Wilberforce
Jeffersonville
Xenia
71
Middletown
Waynesville
22
27
Oregonia
Lebanon
Mason
50
74
Cincinnati
52

Southwest Ohio

SOUTHWEST OHIO

A s the flatlands of central Ohio give way to the rolling hills of the southern part of the state, moods—and accents—change. Part Southern hospitality, part pioneer spirit, the southwestern part of the state has a distinctive charm as well as a distinctive topography. Here you can follow in the footsteps of poets and presidents, retrace the travels of Native American tribes or high-flying inventors, and discover a delightful assortment of small towns and sophisticated big cities.

The anchor of Southwest Ohio is Cincinnati, also known as "The Queen City," where you can go up a lazy river on an American sternwheeler, indulge in some sweet/spicy signature chili, or explore charming neighborhoods and first-class attractions.

WEST LIBERTY

A castle is a strange thing to find straddling the border of Central and Southwest Ohio. But a castle it is—two castles, to be exact, both listed on the National Register of Historic Places. One mile east of West Liberty on State Route 245, not far off I–75, you'll find two of the state's most unusual structures, known collectively as the **Piatt Castles.**

The Shawnee tribe that once inhabited this land called it Mac-A-Cheek. That name later became the name of the home built by Civil War general and gentleman farmer Abram Sanders Piatt, who built his residence of native limestone and hardwoods. Completed in 1868, the thirty-room Norman–French-style chateau is decorated with elaborate woodwork and intricately frescoed ceilings. Castle Mac-A-Cheek is filled with Native American artifacts, antique fire arms, Civil War relics, and fascinating antiques.

Not to be outdone, his brother Donn Piatt, an editor, writer and diplomat, built his own castle, known as Mac-O-Chee (your kids won't be able to resist referring to it as the Mac and Cheese castle in honor of that ever-popular entree). Built in two sections, it was started in the late 1860s as a modest Swiss chalet but was then expanded in the late 1870s with the addition of a Flemish-inspired limestone front. It was completed in 1881.

Individual tours of each structure last forty-five minutes and take in all the secret nooks and crannies. The eleven-room Pioneer House, an 1828 log house that was the brothers' boyhood home and a former stop on the Underground Railroad, now is restored and serves as a country gift and antique shop. Tickets are $5.00 for adults, $3.00 for children age six to twelve. For more information call (513) 465–2821.

Majestic edifices of a more natural kind are the attraction at the **Ohio Caverns,** not far away on Route 245. Bring some sweaters—the temperature year-round is a chilly fifty-four degrees. But your kids won't notice: They'll be too busy oohing and aahing over the pure white stalactites and stalagmites (remember: one grows up, the other down) and skipping ahead through the cavern's lighted passageways. Ohio Caverns are the largest of all Ohio caves and have been billed as "America's most colorful caverns" because the white crystals create a dramatic effect against the red, black, and gray striations of the cave walls.

After the tour unwind with a picnic or a nap in the adjacent thirty-five-acre park while the kids cavort in the playground. Guided tours take about an hour and cover almost a mile of underground walking and climbing. Tours are offered daily from 9:00 A.M. to 5:00 P.M. from April through October, 9:00 A.M. to 4:00 P.M. the rest of the year. Admission is $6.50 for adults, $3.50 for children age five to twelve. The caverns are at 2212 East State Route 245. For more information call (513) 465–4017.

Ohio is widely known as cave country and a spelunker's paradise. Many of these underground adventures are found here in the southwestern part of the state. Here you'll find not just one but two great caverns.

Zane Caverns in nearby Bellefontaine is known for its illuminated stalactites and stalagmites as well as its interesting display of "cave pearls." Cave pearls are formed in pools on the cave's floor when small pieces of gravel or grains of sand are dripped on by calcite and "polished" by water. Zane features rare white pearls.

The caverns reach 132 feet at their deepest point. A forty-minute tour reveals the lore and history of the caves, which were discovered more than a century ago by a hunter whose dog fell into a sinkhole chasing rabbits. Afterward set your little explorers loose in the gift shop, relax at the playground at nearby Bluejacket Campground, or enjoy an above-ground picnic. The caverns are open 10:00 A.M. to 5:00 P.M. daily May through September, weekends only in March, April, October, and November. They're located 6 miles east on State Route 540. Admission is $6.50 for adults, $3.50 for children ages six to twelve. For more information call (513) 592–0891.

The Bellefontaine area is also the site of the state's highest point, nearby 1,550-foot Campbell Hill. So it's not surprising to find **Mad River Mountain,** one of the state's few ski areas, located here.

The mountain has first-class skiing with a lift capacity of 8,400 skiers per hour and snow machines capable of producing five tons of snow per minute. Let your kids loose on the bunny hills while you take to the black-diamond slopes (or vice versa!) and afterward soak those sore muscles at the Mad River Inn. The ski resort is at Road 28, Box 22 in Bellefontaine. For reservations and more information call (513) 599–1015.

A final piece of area trivia: Bellefontaine (French for "beautiful fountain") had the first concrete streets in America, laid out in 1891. Families still drive today on the century-old concrete along Main Street downtown.

PIQUA

You know this section of Ohio doesn't take itself too seriously when it has an annual festival devoted to underwear. Just over the border into Southwest Ohio is Piqua, which honors its "foundations" each year in mid-October. Now in its eighth year, it offers a "brief" but "revealing" glance at the town's history as the "Underwear Capital of the World."

KHRISTI'S TOP FAMILY ADVENTURES IN SOUTHWEST OHIO

1. Paramount King's Island, Mason
2. Museum Center at Union Terminal, Cincinnati
3. Cincinnati Children's Museum, Dayton
4. U.S. Air Force Museum, Dayton
5. Blue Jacket Outdoor Drama, Xenia

In the late 1800s, Piqua had ten factories that turned out hosiery, night-wear, and other undergarments. The last one closed in 1993, but the town has never forgotten its distinguished history. Each year that history takes center stage in the **Great Outdoor Underwear Festival** that crowds the streets of downtown Piqua for two days on the second weekend of October.

Where else can you cheer on competitors in the "Undy 500," participate in the Drop-Seat Trot (a 5-mile run) or the Boxer Ball, even bid at the celebrity underwear auction (Pat Boone, Loni Anderson, and Chubby Checker have participated in the past). There's also the usual festival fare: food booths, entertainment, and more. Admission is free. For information contact (513) 773–1625.

WILBERFORCE

Wilberforce is the home to the **National Afro-American Museum and Cultural Center,** adjacent to Central State University. Open since 1988, this museum and cultural center is a repository for preservation, study, and interpretation. With an ever-expanding collection of artifacts, manuscripts, and archives spread out over more than 35,000 square feet in a contemporary glass and granite building, the museum reflects the traditions, values, social customs, and experiences of African-Americans.

Your children—inheritors of an increasingly diverse world—are sure to gain valuable insights in "From Victory To Freedom: Afro-American Life In The Fifties," an exhibit that chronicles the crucial period in American history from World War II to freedom. The exhibit features the award-winning and toe-tapping presentation, "Music as Metaphor," which traces black music of the period and its influence on American culture. Frequent changing exhibits focus on black history or arts.

The museum is also known for its special events that attract families from all over the state. February features programs in honor of Afro-American History Month; other popular activities include the "Oldie But Goodie" classic car show in the spring, the Holiday Festival of Black Dolls in October, and a Kwanzaa celebration in December. Admission is $3.50 for adults, $1.50 for children. The museum is open 9:00 A.M. to 5:00 P.M. Tuesday through Saturday, 1:00 to 5:00 P.M. Sunday. The museum is at 1350 Brush Row Road; for information call (513) 376–4944.

DAYTON

Dayton was founded in 1796 where four shallow streams meet and was named in honor of General Jonathan Dayton. Some 200 years later, families still wander among original buildings in one of the city's first communities, now known as the **Oregon Historical District.** The twelve-block area along East Fifth Street between Wayne Avenue and Patterson Boulevard is home to antique shops, lively restaurants and pubs, and a well-attended Christmas tour in December that spotlights the area's history and vintage homes.

Dayton is better known as the home to almost 2,000 manufacturing plants and as the birthplace of the Wright brothers. Orville and Wilbur's original laboratory has been moved to Greenfield Village in Dearborn, Michigan, but Dayton visitors can still see Orville Wright's home in Oakwood at Harmon and Park avenues as well as other Wright-related memorabilia in the city's museums and historic areas.

Do your kids think Wilbur and Orville Wright make popcorn? Help their imaginations soar with a visit to the city's **Carillon Historical Park.** The Wright Flyer III, in which Orville and Wilbur taught themselves to fly, is one of the many treasures at this sixty-five-acre villagelike outdoor museum of history, transportation, and invention.

Besides the many aviation-related artifacts, there are antique autos, a fancy railroad car, and a replica of the Wright brothers' bicycle shop. Highlights include a 1905 Wright brothers' airplane, a 1930s print shop, and a ninety-seven-year-old schoolhouse. Dayton's oldest building, the 1796 Newcom Tavern, is also here. The park is named for the stately, fifty-bell carillon that towers over the grounds. Admission is a bargain at $1.00 per adult; free for children. The park is located at 2001 South Patterson Boulevard and is open Tuesday through Saturday from 10:00 A.M. to 6:00 P.M., Sunday from 1:00 to 6:00 P.M. from May 1 through October 31. For more information call (513) 293-2841.

The Wright stuff is also seen at the **Wright Cycle Company and Hoover Block,** off West Third Street. This bike shop is where Wilbur and Orville combined their bicycle business with their first career, printing, in 1895. While working there they manufactured their first bikes and began their early work in aviation that led to the first flight some seven years later. The bike shop was declared a National Historic Landmark in 1990 and includes historic photographs, artifacts, and more. The nearby Hoover Block building once housed their business, "Wright & Wright Job Printing," which printed some of the work of another Dayton luminary, poet Paul Laurence Dunbar. The shop is at 22 South Williams Street and is open daily in summer, weekends only in winter. For hours and more information call (513) 443-0793.

If your amateur aviators are interested in other Wright landmarks, the National Park Service recently established a **Dayton Heritage National Historical Park** to honor the Wrights' legacy and the work of their friend Dunbar. A free guide to the park's historic buildings and the city's Aviation Trail is available through the Convention and Visitors Bureau, 1 Chamber Plaza, Suite A, Dayton, 45402 (513-226-8248).

Ever seen a fire-breathing, four-story-tall, airplane-eating monster robot? Sights like this are commonplace at the spectacular **Dayton Air Show,** held each July at the city's International Airport in Vandalia. An action-packed weekend of aviation adventures starts at 7:00 A.M. with thundering jets, incredible aerobatics, barnstormers, sky divers, air racing, balloons, explosive pyrotechnics, and more. The Dayton Air Show is the leading event of its kind in North America, drawing more than 250,000 people and 150 types of aircraft annually. For dates and more information call (800) 848–3699.

Hitch a ride on the back of a giant dragonfly, drift over Niagara Falls in a hot-air balloon, wing walk over the Grand Canyon, experience the last big San Francisco earthquake, or soar over the walls of a castle in France on a set of wings constructed of just feathers. The dynamics of natural and mechanical flight are the focus of the breathtaking IMAX theatre at the **U.S. Air Force Museum,** the oldest and largest military-aviation museum in the world.

The 60-by 80-foot theater is like no other movie palace you've ever seen. The giant screen is as high as a six-story building and projects an image that's three times larger than a standard movie. The dynamic sound system is among the best modern technology has produced. This, in combination with a steeply inclined auditorium, gives your family the feeling of being in the middle of the action. Films change regularly and are screened seven days a week on the hour from 10:00 A.M. to 5:00 P.M.

But that's not all there is to experience at this incredible museum. Located on the Wright–Patterson Air Force Base about 5 miles northeast of downtown Dayton, the museum is also the most popular free attraction in the state. Some ten acres of outstanding exhibits span the history of flight from hot air balloons to the B-1 bomber and attract some 1.6 million visitors each year.

Highlights include the famous British Sopwith Camel, a classic aircraft from World War I, one-of-a-kind planes including the North American XB-70 "Valkyrie," an original Wright wind tunnel, and the original Apollo 15 command module. If all this seems a little overwhelming to your kids, steer them toward the "Discovery Hangar Five," a newly opened interactive exhibit that focuses on the hows and whys of flight and teaches children about the different types of airplanes, the parts of a plane, and how they work.

The museum is on Springfield Street (State Route 444) at Gate 28B, Wright–Patterson Air Force Base. Hours are 9:00 A.M. to 5:00 P.M. daily. Admission is free. For more information call (513) 255–3284.

After a visit to most aviation museums your daughter may feel that women have had little—if any—role in the exploration of air and space. If so take her to the **International Women's Air and Space Museum,** off I–675, which honors women's role in aviation and space history. Located in an early nineteenth-century limestone house in Centerville, a Dayton suburb, this small but fascinating museum gives equal time to women aviators such as Amelia Earhart, Jacqueline Cochran, the women astronauts, and the more recent women of Desert Storm. A special display honors Katharine Wright, Wilbur and Orville's sister. Katharine has been mostly forgotten, but Orville once said, "When the world speaks of the Wrights, it must include my sister, for much of our effort has been inspired by her."

The museum is located in the restored Asahel Wright House, the former home of Wilbur and Orville's great uncle. It's open only on Saturdays from 10:00 A.M. to 4:00 P.M. and admission is free. The museum is located at 26 North Main Street, Centerville, 45459 (513–433–6766).

Perhaps the Wrights were inspired by the many wild birds that called the Dayton area home. Today the descendants of those birds are found in the **Aullwood Audubon Center and Farm** on Aullwood Road. This 200-acre wildlife refuge and educational farm lets your kids get up close and personal with more than 200 examples of animal, bird, and plant life. Five miles of trails meander through streams, woods, and meadows and make a hearty hike for even fit families. A hands-on nature center allow children to learn at their own pace or identify one of the center's many bird varieties. The farm is at 1000 Aullwood Road in suburban Vandalia; hours are 9:00 A.M. to 5:00 P.M. Monday through Saturday, 1:00 to 5:00 P.M. Sunday. Tickets are $3.00 for adults, $2.00 for children. For information call (513) 890–7360.

Your kids will be seeing stars at the new planetarium, part of the **Dayton Museum of Natural History.** The museum's innovative Space Theater has a planetarium with a state-of-the-art Digistar system that guides visitors on computerized star treks throughout the universe.

During a visit your family will discover secrets of the natural world from across continents or in your own backyard. Travel back in time to see the tools, jewelry, and other artifacts of the peoples that inhabited the Miami Valley 14,000 years ago. Explore an Egyptian tomb, peek into the rocky den of VanCleve, the museum's resident bobcat, or take a walk on the wild side during a visit to the Wild Ohio Zoo, which features more than fifty animals native to the Buckeye State in their own habitat.

The museum is at 26000 DeWeese Parkway, just north of downtown off I–75. Hours are 9:00 A.M. to 5:00 P.M. Tuesday, Wednesday, Thursday, and Saturday; 9:00 A.M. to 9:00 P.M. Friday, noon to 5:00 P.M. Sunday. The museum is closed Monday. Admission is $3.00 for adults, $1.50 for children age three to sixteen. For more information call (513) 275–7431.

Feel like almost everything in Dayton is related to exploration of air and space? Come back to earth with a visit to the **Dayton Art Institute,** where inspiration takes a more concrete form. This museum, which looks remarkably like an Italian villa and towers over the city on a nearby hill, has noteworthy examples of European painting and a stunning East Asian wing. Its holdings represent more than 10,000 objects spanning 5,000 years.

Of special interest to families is the Experiencenter, where you can encourage your young Van Goghs. This hands-on area—including more than twenty activities just for kids—prompts visitors to interact with art and experiment with the basic elements of line, pattern, color, texture, and shape.

The museum is at Forest and Riverview avenues and is open 9:00 A.M. to 5:00 P.M. Monday through Sunday. Admission is free. For more information call (513) 223–5277.

Most re-created historic villages trace Ohio's roots to the Colonial era or the nineteenth-century. **Sun Watch Thirteenth-Century Indian Village** takes your family back a few moccasin-clad steps further into the world of an 800-year-old Native American village.

Some 800 years ago, a group of Ohio's early farmers, now known as the Fort Ancient Indians, settled along the banks of the Great Miami River. More than twenty years of excavation was completed before the village was constructed; today it consists of thatched huts surrounded by a stockade. In recognition of its significance, Sun Watch was designated a National Historic Landmark in 1990.

During a visit your kids will learn how to tell time based on an ancient, complex system of charting the sun; discover how archaeologists pieced together the fragments of their finds to create a rich and complex culture; and see how the village's ancient inhabitants used bone, skin, and stone to create beautiful and useful objects. Tours include the Big House, where Indian councils were held, and life-sized dioramas that display unearthed artifacts. Special seasonal events celebrate planting and the harvest; the diversity of Native American culture and the annual homage to summer; and a weekend of traditional dancing, music, craft demonstrations, and more.

Sun Watch is at 2301 West River Road in Dayton, just south of downtown on I–75. Hours are 9:00 A.M. to 5:00 P.M. Monday through Saturday, noon to 5:00 P.M. Sundays. The village is open year-round but closed Mondays from November 1 through March 31. Admission is $4.00 for adults, $3.00 for children ages six to seventeen; free for ages five and younger. For more information call (513) 268–8199.

More recent—but no less fascinating—history is found at the **Dunbar House.** Think your kids are little geniuses? Although born into a life of poverty, African-American poet Paul Laurence Dunbar wrote his first poem at age six and recited publicly at age nine. He later edited the school newspaper, wrote for various Dayton-area newspapers, and published his first book of poetry at the ripe old age of twenty. He counted among his friends the Wright Brothers, Booker T. Washington, and Frederick Douglass.

Dunbar was the first African-American writer to gain acceptance in national and international literary circles. He later moved to Washington, became a prominent speaker about Civil Rights issues and found fame, if not fortune. A longtime sufferer of tuberculosis, he died at just thirty-three but continues to serve as inspiration to millions today.

Dunbar's home in Dayton has been restored to appear as it did when he lived there, including rooms furnished with his own possessions. On display are Dunbar's bike built by the Wright Brothers, the desk and chair where he composed much of his work, his collection of Native American art, and—the favorite of young boy visitors—a ceremonial sword presented to Dunbar by President Teddy Roosevelt. The Dunbar house is on Third Street in Dayton and is open year-round. For more information and hours call (513) 224–7061.

XENIA

The epic struggle between the Shawnee Indians who called this area home and the frontiersmen who arrived to claim it as their own provides plenty of exciting action at the **Blue Jacket Outdoor Drama** held June through

September at the 1,200-seat Caesar's Ford Park Amphitheater.

Blue Jacket is the true story of a white man adopted into the Shawnee Indian Nation who in the late 1700s became their war chief. You'll share Blue Jacket's friendship with the warrior, Caesar, and their struggle to protect the Shawnee homeland against frontiersmen such as Daniel Boone and Simon Kenton.

The first performance was staged in 1982. It takes more than fifty actors, a dozen horses, more than 1,000 costume pieces, and dazzling pyrotechnics and special effects to make this story come alive. Shows are held at 8:00 P.M. nightly except Mondays; tickets are $10–$12 for adults, $6.00 for children. A dinner buffet is also available for $6.95 ($5.95 for children) as are twice-daily backstage tours. For more information call (513) 376–4318.

MASON

The 330-foot replica of the Eiffel Tower rising from the rolling hills and Ohio farmland not far from Cincinnati is disconcerting at first. Then you realize that this French fantasy is right at home among all of the others at this king of amusement parks in southern Ohio. A trip to Paris? *Bien sûr!* A ride into space on the Starship *Enterprise?* Beam me up, Scotty. Anything seems possible here.

Each year **Paramount King's Island** tries to top itself with new shows and a new ride that's designed to be faster and scarier than the one introduced the year before. But it's going to take quite a thriller to unseat the current king of this island—better known as "The Beast."

It's even listed in the *Guinness Book of World Records.* With 7,400 feet of track, the ominous Beast is the longest wooden roller coaster in the world. The ride lasts three minutes and forty seconds, with riders reaching a maximum speed of almost 65 miles per hour. Almost as frightening is the Vortex, which sends screaming riders through six hair-raising upside-down loops before bringing them to a crashing halt. (*Warning:* These roller coasters may be too stressful for young children.)

Want to keep your feet planted firmly on *terra firma?* No problem. Visitors who choose to skip the scream machines can get wet and wild at the water park. A family favorite, it includes sixteen water slides, includ-

Venture into Hanna–Barbera Land at Paramount King's Island and you never know who you'll meet! (Courtesy King's Island)

ing white-water rafting. Or you can choose from more than 100 other rides, many of them refreshingly tame. Paramount King's Island is the largest seasonal theme park in the Midwest and has something for everyone.

Tiny thrill seekers can meet their favorite cartoon characters and get a hug from Yogi or Scooby-Doo at Hanna–Barbera Land or enter the three-acre world of television with Nickelodeon, the newest area for children. Dare your kids to solve the Green Slime maze—but be prepared: They're sure to get dirty. You never know what's behind the next turn or how wet your kids will get as they wind their way through. Afterward, stop by the Gak Kitchen for a tasty—if unappealing sounding—sample of the Gakmeister's latest, gooiest creation. Or be a part of the ooze in Mega Mess-a-Mania, a game show featuring stunts and challenges from hit Nickelodeon game shows. For the more traditional minded, Coney Mall has all the sights, sounds, and smells of an old-fashioned amusement park. The park is 24 miles north of Cincinnati. Two-day passes are available. For more information and current admission prices call (800) 288–0808.

Across from King's Island is the Midwest's largest waterpark, also known as **The Beach.** Endless summer is the attraction here, where your family can catch a real wave at the Thunder Beach wavepool, float along the Lazy Miami River on a 1½ mile ride with a riverboat motif, or brave The Twilight Zoom, a double-tube water slide that ends with an exciting splashdown.

Afterward, boogie to Jamaican tunes played by a live reggae band, cavort on more than thirty water slides and attractions, or relax on 40,000 sprawling square feet of beach—more than enough for a few impressive sandcastles. With thirty-five acres and two million gallons of wild waves, the park is the perfect wild and watery family escape. There's even Splash Mountain for the little squirts—with lots of warm water and pint-sized play areas. The *New York Times*—which seldom writes much about the Midwest—named it "one of America's 10 best waterparks."

The park is open daily May through September and is located at 2590 Waterpark Drive in Mason. Hours in season are 10:00 A.M. to 7:00 P.M. For current ticket prices and more information call (800) 886–SWIM or (513) 398–SWIM.

MIDDLETOWN

A visit to the huge, sprawling King's Island may leave you wondering if any old-fashioned amusement parks—the kind you remember from your childhood—still exist. They do, and one is located not far from the hustle and bustle of King's Island in peaceful Middletown, 30 miles north of Cincinnati.

At **Americana Amusement Park** your family can kick back and wander among the classic rides, including three roller coasters, sixteen kiddie rides, and live stage shows or don your suits and dog-paddle in the Olympic-size swimming pool. Afterward check out the petting zoo or the Jolly Roger play area, hop a ride on the train or the showboat or just slip off your shoes and pull up a blanket for a picnic in the park's 10,000-seat picnic grove. Seasonal hours are 11:00 A.M. to 8:00 P.M. daily. The park is on State Route 4 in Middletown; for more information and rates call (513) 539–7339.

LEBANON

Settled in 1796 and rich in history, Lebanon is home to the state's oldest inn and restaurant as well as more than forty charming antique and specialty shops. **The Golden Lamb,** which dates to 1803, has hosted ten U.S. presidents and various worldwide luminaries. George Washington may not have slept here, but you can put your feet up in the same room (and in some cases, the same bed) where Charles Dickens or Samuel Clemens (Mark Twain) laid their hallowed heads. The inn's eighteen rooms are named after the famous people who slept there. (Interestingly enough, Dickens was less than complimentary when he visited the United States in 1842; only later did innkeeper Calvin Bradley discover that the "small, rather disagreeable man" who eloquently bellowed his less than favorable opinions about America to anyone who would listen was the illustrious author of *A Christmas Carol* and other classics.)

Even if you choose not to stay in one of the rooms, your family can absorb a little of the area's rich history with a meal in one of the famous dining rooms. There are four public and five private dining areas. The specialty in each is all-American—from Yankee pot roast and tasty turkey with mashed potatoes to old-fashioned apple pie and other home-baked desserts.

On Sundays local families crowd the tables to celebrate birthdays and anniversaries, so reservations are a good idea.

Unoccupied rooms are always open for inspection. While there head up to the fourth floor, where you can check out a series of guest rooms decorated with Shaker and period furnishings—one is known as "Sarah's Room" and furnished for Sarah Stubbs, who lived at the inn as a child. The room is a little girl's dream—complete with a nostalgic collection of furniture and toys that will have any child itching to step inside.

The Golden Lamb is at 27 South Broadway. For more information call (513) 932–5065.

If you saved room for dessert, a good place to have it is the **Village Ice Cream Parlor** across the street. This ice cream parlor is so quintessential that even Hollywood has discovered it—it had a supporting role in both *Harper Valley P.T.A.* with Barbara Eden and the more recent film, *Milk Money* with Ed Harris and Melanie Griffith. With wire chairs, ceiling fans, and specialties that include a Shaker Sundae (vanilla, chocolate, and strawberry ice cream topped with chocolate, butterscotch, and strawberry syrups, cherries and nuts), it'll have you dieting for weeks afterward.

OREGONIA

Southwest of Lebanon the awesome earthworks at **Fort Ancient State Memorial** are an important North American archaeological site. On a bluff rising some 240 feet above the Little Miami River, the prehistoric Hopewell Indians (circa 100 B.C.–A.D. 500) constructed more than 3½ miles of earth and stone walls now known as Fort Ancient. The 100-acre enclosure, one of the nation's finest examples of a Hopewell hilltop community, is now a National Historic Landmark.

While there you may see kids of all ages sifting through the dirt of a mock archaeological site as part of the site's popular "Digging The Past" program. It is believed that the site was used both for defense and as a gathering place for social and religious ceremonies.

Families can learn about both groups at the on-site museum, which contains archaeological artifacts and more. Exhibits here explore Hopewell and Fort Ancient artifacts and culture. Afterward pull on your hiking boots and explore the Earthworks Trail, which stretches for about a mile and offers two scenic overlooks with two clear views of the earthworks. There's also a comfortable picnic area, perfect for an open-air snack or meal.

Fort Ancient is at 6123 State Route 350 in Oregonia. Hours vary by season. For more information call (513) 932–4421.

WAYNESVILLE

This tiny town—home to the first Stetson hat and to more than 35 tempting antique shops, earning it the nickname "Antiques Capital of the Midwest"—attracts thousands of revelers to the area during two annual festivals. Each year it pays homage to an unlikely pair: cabbages and kings.

Ever seen the movie *Brigadoon?* Willy-Nilly-on-the-Wash, although less melodic, is a town like Brigadoon that only exists for a short time. On weekends from late August through mid-October, the sixteenth-century town appears magically on more than thirty acres just east of downtown on State Road 73 (technically in Harveysburg). At the annual **Ohio Renaissance Festival** your kids can speak with Shakespeare, juggle with a jester, even crack open a dragon egg.

More than 150 costumed peasants, pirates, merchants, and royalty (even a few serfs and fools) bring the era to life. There's a joust three times daily, complete with clanking armor and flying pennants. Here your family can wander among the wares of more than 130 merchants selling everything from shields to stone sculpture, dance the jig around the maypole, learn the art of swordplay and chivalry, and afterward sample the hearty food and drink of the age at one of many food stands. For even more fun, schedule a visit during one of the special theme weekends in September and October, when the classic tale of Robin Hood comes alive or the Queen celebrates her birthday, or when games of skill challenge visitors and villagers at the Highland Games. Huzzah!

The festival is held yearly from late August through mid-October. For current ticket prices and hours contact (513) 897–7000.

Like your fun on the sour side? Pucker up and chow down during the two-day **Ohio Sauerkraut Festival,** held each year the second full weekend in October. You may have heard of sauerkraut on a hot dog, but you'll be amazed at all the other culinary uses for this cabbagey creation.

Watch noble knights in full armor joust in a Tournament of Honor three times daily at the Ohio Renaissance Festival, held annually from late August through mid-October. (Courtesy Ohio Renaissance Festival)

Ever try sauerkraut fudge? How 'bout sauerkraut pizza? Here's your chance. Even doughnuts and cream pies get a dollop of kraut at the booths that line Main Street during this festive event, now in its twenty-sixth year. Strangely enough, Waynesville has no special ties to this food specialty: The festival began because a local businessman who wanted to start up a local fall festival had sauerkraut for lunch.

Besides sampling sauerkraut, your family can browse and buy from the arts and crafts of more than 400 craftspeople who line the street, enjoy continuous entertainment, and just people watch among the more than 250,000 kraut cravers of all ages who flock to this charming town. Admission is free. For more information call the Waynesville Chamber of Commerce at (513) 897–8855.

CINCINNATI

Winston Churchill once called Cincinnati "the most beautiful of America's inland cities." This big city perched high on the bluffs of the Ohio River is known for its small-town charm. It also has a vibrant and exciting downtown, with a twenty-block elevated skywalk system connecting department stores, specialty shops, restaurants, hotels, and even a museum. It's also as far south as you can go in the state without hitting the bluegrass of Kentucky, located just across the river.

Your family is sure to agree with Churchill after a visit to "The Queen City." From the first professional fire department (and a museum honoring it) to the equally fiery and famous Skyline Chili, known 'round the world, this is one hot and happenin' city.

A good place to get a grip on the city's psyche is downtown's **Fountain Square,** where the *Genius of Water* sculpture atop the Tyler Davidson Fountain surveys a broad, open plaza. In sunny weather you'll find shoppers and businesspeople "brown-bagging" it on the square or enjoying some famous chili while being entertained by performances on the open-air pavilion stage. The plaza is also home to the **Cincy Shop,** where your family can find maps, books, guides and virtually any Cincinnati-related item your hearts could desire.

What would Chicago and Paris be without the Sears and Eiffel Towers? Cincy has its own nosebleed section at the top of the **Carew Tower**

Observatory, nearby at Fifth and Vine streets. From the top of the city's tallest building you'll be treated to excellent views of downtown as well as the surrounding metropolitan area, complete with rolling hills and Kentucky in the near distance. Carew also connects to other city shopping and sites. The observatory is open Monday through Friday from 9:30 A.M. to 5:30 P.M., 10:00 A.M. to 4:45 P.M. Saturday, and 11:00 A.M. to 4:45 P.M. Sunday. Admission is $2.00 for adults, $1.00 for children. Call (513) 579–9735.

Other great views of the city can be had at one of the scenic over-looks in **Eden Park,** part of the stylish, high-rent Mt. Adams neighborhood. When the skyscrapers and the bustle get to be too much, city residents of all ages retreat to this well-used greensward. This sprawling park boasts many of Cincy's most popular attractions, including its renowned art museum, two professional theaters, and miles and miles of trails perfect for walking, hiking, biking or rollerblading (just remember to wear pads; the hills can be steep!).

If you prefer, your family can choose a little slower pace with a stroll around the eighty-eight galleries of the **Cincinnati Art Museum.** This was the first museum west of the Alleghenies built to be a museum; today its graceful halls house art dating back some 5,000 years. Founded in 1881, the museum opened to world acclaim and was heralded as "The Art Palace of the West."

Not one to rest on its laurels, the museum has just completed the most extensive renovation in its more than 100-year history. Today the collection and the museum's hilltop location still enchant visitors of all ages.

The medieval arms and armor—especially the sharp-edge pole arms—look as menacing as they were intended to, but kids love them. They also love the old musical instruments, the huge untitled mural by Joan Miro (it originally hung in the restaurant of the city's Terrace Plaza Hotel and was later given to the museum), and the colorful *Red Rooster* by Marc Chagall. Mary Cassatt's poignant *Mother and Child* from 1889 will leave you wistful for your children's babyhood.

Steering wheels, hubcaps, refrigerator doors, ancient TV cabinets, radio tubes—they're all art up in the contemporary galleries, where kids will be mesmerized by Korean sculptor Nam June Paik's futuristic robot entitled *Powel Crosley, Jr.* The whimsical work pays homage to the televi-

TOP ANNUAL EVENTS
IN SOUTHWEST OHIO

Cincinnati Flower Show, April, Cincinnati; (513) 579–0259
Taste of Cincinnati, May, Cincinnati; (513) 579–3199
Kids Fest, June, Cincinnati; (513) 352–4000
National Folk Festival, June, Dayton; (513) 223–3655
U.S. Air & Trade Show, July, Dayton; (513) 898–5901
Ohio Renaissance Festival, August through October, Waynesville;
    (513) 897–7000
Oktoberfest Zinzinnati, September, Cincinnati;
    (513) 528–9400
Ohio Sauerkraut Festival, October, Waynesville;
    (513) 897–8855

sion age and was commissioned by the museum in honor of Crosley, a father of modern telecommunications and onetime owner of the Cincinnati Reds. Baseball fans flock to Andy Warhol's baseball-card-style tribute to Cincinnati Reds great Pete Rose.

Other museum favorites include six paintings of Indians and settlers by artist Henry Farny, works by local artist Frank Duveneck (including his most famous, *Whistling Boy,* which may have your kids puckering up and attempting a tune while you stand in front of it. Interestingly enough research has shown that the boy isn't quite as innocent as he appears: He's really smoking, not whistling), and the extensive collection of Cincinnati-made Rookwood pottery. From ancient Egyptian to the more modern Expressionist school, there's something here for art lovers of all ages and interests.

The museum offers family-fun tours every Saturday at 1:00 and 3:00 P.M. when admission is free and on Sundays at 2:00 P.M. There's also a monthly special program, "For Curious Kids," which explores the wonders of the permanent collection and encourages creative thinking. The museum is open Tuesday through Saturday from 10:00 A.M. to 5:00 P.M. Museum admission is $5.00 for adults; free for children under age eighteen. For more information call (513) 721–5204.

Not far away, also in Eden Park, is the **Krohn Conservatory,** one of the nation's largest public greenhouses. Here your little green thumbs can adventure into the exotic world of tropical and desert plants and learn about horticulture firsthand. Wander through a tropical rain forest, walk under a spectacular twenty-foot waterfall, or dry out in the desert greenhouse filled with prickly cacti and fabulous, delicate orchids. All of Cincy gathers for the seasonal events, which include festive holiday floral shows. The conservatory is open daily from 10:00 A.M. to 5:00 P.M. For hours and more information call (513) 421–4086.

The neighborhood known as Mt. Adams is also one of the city's liveliest. It's often compared to San Francisco, as much for its annoying one-way streets as its breathtaking hilltop views. Here you'll find narrow row houses, most restored to their former nineteenth-century glory, as well as funky shops and interesting restaurants.

Among the most interesting is the **Rookwood Pottery Restaurant,** housed in the former pottery of the same name. Rookwood, active from around the turn of the century through the 1930s, is known for its intricate glazes and beautiful designs. It is highly prized by today's collectors. Your kids will love the chance to sit inside one of the three huge brick kilns (once reaching thousands of degrees) while dining on the burgers voted the best in the city by *Cincinnati* magazine (like almost every other restaurant in the city, they also boast their own brand of chili). Vintage photographs, original pieces of pottery, and a great make-your-own sundae bar add to the ambience. The restaurant is at 1077 Celestial Street; call (513) 721–5456.

Not far from the restaurant is the **Cincinnati Playhouse in the Park,** one of the city's intimate theaters. With just over 600 seats in the Circular Theater and 230 in the Shelterhouse theater, they are known for offering unusual plays and family favorites. There's also a great view of the city from the parking lot, as well as a few well-used picnic tables that are perfect for a relaxing snack or meal. For ticket and schedule information call the box office at (513) 421–3888.

Have your kids ever wanted to slide down a fire pole? They'll get their chance at the **Cincinnati Fire Museum,** a restored 1907 fire station where they can also test their strength and endurance by having a go at a replica of a hand-pumped engine. The city is known for being the site of the nation's first professional fire department—founded in the 1850s—and this museum touches on topics from bucket brigades to fire prevention in a way that's both educational and entertaining. There's even a wooden fire hose. Hours are 10:00 A.M. to 4:00 P.M. weekdays; noon to 4:00 P.M. weekends. The museum is at 315 West Court Street. For more information call (513) 621–5553.

Some cities choose to honor their past by tearing it down piece by piece in the name of progress. This is not so in preservation-minded Cincinnati, which, when faced with an unused Art Deco train station the size of fourteen football fields, decided to turn it into not one but three fantastic museums.

Union Terminal was built in 1933 and once hosted up to 216 trains and 34,000 people daily. It closed in 1972, victim of America's love affair with the automobile. Now restored to its original grandeur, it stands as one of the country's most spectacular remaining examples of streamlined Art Deco architecture, with a magnificent soaring rotunda filled with murals and distinctive Deco details.

Today this extraordinary cultural center on Western Avenue is a prime example of adaptive reuse. Inside the bright, soaring space—it covers 500,000 square feet—you'll find three family favorites: the **Cincinnati Museum of Natural History,** the **Cincinnati Historical Society,** and the **Robert D. Lindner Family Omnimax Theater.** All together, they're known as the **Museum Center at Cincinnati Union Terminal.**

For an overview of the city's long and lively history, check out the Cincinnati Historical Society first. Here your family can trace the Queen City's development from frontier river town to modern metropolis.

Costumed interpreters escort you and your kids on a journey through time, from a frontier cabin to a 1940s-era gas station. "Cincinnati: From Settlement to 1860" chronicles the city's founding and the often demanding pioneer lifestyle. Visit a settler's cabin and experience the rousing drum rolls and battle cries at Fort Washington.

As you move through the re-created streets of nineteenth-century Cincy, you'll hear boosters praise the city's past and future. Your kids will love the chance to learn about the area's agricultural products by moving wooden boats along a 50-foot model of the Miami and Erie Canals. River life is also the spotlight in the "La Belle Riviere" section, where your gang can board an old-fashioned flatboat (a plaque nearby calls it the "moving van of the frontier"), talk to a "real" pioneer family, and watch lively programs on river life.

The river and the historical role it played in city history are also chronicled in "Queen City of the West," where you can imagine the thrill of a steamboat ride as you step on board a 94-foot side-wheel steamboat or stroll an entire block of nineteenth-century shops. The modern era is represented by "Cincinnati Goes to War." Spark young imaginations with a visit to a full-size gas station from the era and an authentic World War II broadcast studio. Kids can even climb aboard an original 1923 trolley that was used in the city until 1951 and take an imaginary ride through the streets of vintage Cincy.

The museum frequently hosts special family-style exhibits. Past favorites have included a display revolving around the role of the circus in American history (complete with free popcorn, face painting, and a huge miniature circus under the big top); planned in 1996 is an exhibit tracing the influence of "Star Trek" on American culture.

Just steps away, the Cincinnati Museum of Natural History captivates visitors of all ages. There's a special emphasis here on the natural and geological history of the Ohio Valley. Don't be surprised if the guides seem young—the museum's innovative "Lab Rats" program turns high school students into knowledgeable guides who perform scientific demonstrations and answer visitors' questions.

First stop: the Ice Age. Travel back 19,000 years in time to an era when ice covered the Ohio Valley. Walk through a mock glacier (better bring a sweater!) and feel the spine-tingling chill of living in a time when one-ton ground sloths and saber-toothed tigers roamed the earth. Afterward go underground and navigate the narrow twists and turns in "The Cavern," a simulated Kentucky limestone cave, complete with underground waterfalls, streams, fossils, and even a live bat colony (safely contained behind glass, of course).

Are your preschoolers bored with Barney? Let them experience the real thing in Dinosaur Hall, where interactive games and puzzles surround a dino exhibit and where they can have a hand at digging up a dinosaur bone using brushes and archaeological tools. A display extolling the virtues of recycling shows the incredible amount of garbage an average family of four uses in a week, as well as innovative and easy ways to reduce it.

Finally, turn the kids loose in the Children's Discovery Center, with two major hands-on areas. "All About You" teaches kids about the inner workings of the body; "Pathways to Change" lets them travel through time to learn how people through the ages have changed and adapted to their environment. Here they can brush a huge set of teeth, play Captain Digesto pinball (it traces the path food takes through the digestive system), and pretend to be a doctor or dentist in the kid-sized offices.

Don't leave Museum Center without stopping at the Omnimax Theater, which takes movies to new heights. There's no popcorn, but your local multiplex will pale in comparison to this five-story, 72-foot-wide domed screen.

This spectacular facility—the only such theater in the region—wraps your family in a hypersensory experience. Special technology enables you to experience every scene and motion with gut-wrenching, eye-popping clarity. The camera lets you zoom through dramatic, panoramic settings around the world and beyond from the comfort of your seat.

Movies change frequently. Past films have explored man's "Destiny In Space," the natural wonders of "Yellowstone," and have even gone "To The Max" with the Rolling Stones.

Other Museum Center attractions include the Art Collection of the Cincinnati Public Schools, with 97 paintings by nineteenth- and twentieth-century local artists; The Arts Consortium, with a changing art exhibit gallery and a high-tech journey though Cincy's black history; and the Newsreel Theater, which shows World War II newsreels and is free to the public. Train lovers of all ages can experience the romance of the rails with a visit to the Radio Control Tower, originally used for train traffic control. Now restored by the Cincinnati Railroad Club, it's open Saturdays from 10:00 A.M. to 4:00 P.M. and Tuesdays and Thursdays from 8:00 A.M. to 11:00 P.M.

Feeling hungry? Chow down on chili or refuel with a sweet treat in the **Rookwood Ice Cream Parlor,** with glowing walls and floors of authentic area-made Rookwood tile. Afterward stop and shop. Three Museum Center shops—the Collector's Shop at the Cincinnati Museum of Natural History, and the Children's Shop and the Heritage Shop at the Cincinnati Historical Society sell gifts and goods that make great souvenirs of your visit.

One admission ticket ($12 for adults, $7.00 for ages three to twelve) includes admission to all Museum Center attractions. Hours are 9:00 A.M. to 5:00 P.M. Monday through Saturday, 11:00 A.M. to 6:00 P.M. Sunday. Omnimax shows are Monday through Friday beginning at 1:00 P.M., Saturday and Sunday beginning at 11:00 A.M. The Museum Center is at 1301 Western Avenue. For more information call (513) 287-7000.

More fun tailored to small fry can be had at the **Children's Museum of Cincinnati,** a new and welcome addition to the city's museum scene. Just an infant at one year old, it has already attracted a loyal following of local and out-of-town kids and their parents.

Located in a restored train warehouse (you can watch trains snake their way overhead from the museum's parking lot), the brightly colored space is guarded by a huge yellow, purple, and blue dragon that hangs playfully over the entrance. Don't let him deter you, however.

Once inside you'll have a hard time holding on to the kids, who will be tempted to run off on their own to try the more than 200 hands-on activities spread out over three floors. Infants crawl to the Baby Beach, where they can stick plastic fish to an imaginary water wall, fish in a shallow pond filled with real water, and man a boat or watch workers make huge bubbles on a "bubble barge." Preschoolers prefer Kids Cove, with its "Art a la Carte" station, where they can pull on a smock and explore their artistic side using shells, markers, and glue.

The second floor holds even more delightful discoveries. Among them are "Media Dimensions," with a TV studio where your would-be anchormen and women or sitcom stars can dress up and watch themselves on a small screen; "Shapes Relate," with a huge mirrored cube that they can walk through; and "The Works," with an imaginary candy factory (complete with film clips from the old "I Love Lucy" program) where they can work with a conveyer belt and try to keep up with mass production.

And there's more. "Invention Central" lets them build a castle with Popsicle sticks, learn to weave or operate miniature dump trucks and construction machines. "Where in the World Are You?" offers clues that help kids learn about other cultures as well as a huge foam puzzle of the United States (do they know where Ohio is?). And don't miss the chance to take a picture of your child in one of the many costumes from different countries.

The third floor is devoted to energy and sounds. Here kids can play a huge electric harp, try their hand at a sound effects generator, or pluck, beat, rub, shake, blow or strum one of a handful of instruments in the "Sounds Around" area in order to make music. Afterward have a snack in the drive-in diner, also located on the third floor, or splurge in the great first-floor gift shop.

Admission is $6.00 for ages six to adult; those age five and younger pay their age in dollars. Hours are noon to 5:00 P.M. Wednesday, Thursday, and Sunday; noon to 8:00 P.M. Friday; 10:00 A.M. to 5:00 P.M. Saturday. The museum is at 700 West Pete Rose Way, Cincinnati, 45203. For more information call (513) 421–5437.

Dinnertime? Let the family rest their feet and refuel at the **Old Spaghetti Factory** before heading back downtown. Just a few steps away from the Children's Museum, it's known for its kid-friendly atmosphere and menu, including many perennially popular pasta choices. And don't leave Cincinnati without tasting its world-famous chili, served on almost every street corner. The Queen City has more chili joints than any other place in the world. **Camp Washington Chili,** open twenty-four hours, was even immortalized in a song and featured on national network news.

Cincinnati chili parlors such as **Skyline** and **Gold Star,** along with a number of independent local shops, dispense gallons of secret-recipe chili spiked with cinnamon and allspice (the spices are due to the chili's Greek origins). Cincy chili is unlike any other you've tasted. It's served three-way (ladled over spaghetti on a small platter and topped with mild cheddar cheese); four-way (add kidney beans or chopped onions) or five-way (add both). Oyster crackers are served on the side. The hot stuff even has its own festival, held downtown along West Court Street for two days at the end of September.

After heating up with some chili (it's popular any time of year), cool down and get some fresh air at the **Bicentennial Commons at Sawyer Point,** one of the city's newest and most beloved parks. Built in honor of the city's bicentennial, it skirts the river and boasts an impressive roster of recreation facilities and scenic overlooks. When entering, look up to see the Cincinnati Gateway Sculpture, a whimsical, three-dimensional work that pays homage to the city's history. (Interestingly enough, the sculpture was also quite controversial. Many residents were offended by the bronze winged pigs—a reference to the city's onetime nickname "Porkopolis" because of its pork industry—but many loved them, and today they stand as a playful reminder to residents not to take themselves too seriously.)

While there, why not take a turn at the 21,000-square-foot roller-skating pavilion, a favorite of the city's in-line enthusiasts, join in a game of sand volleyball, or just wander the 4-mile Riverwalk, where you can trace the city's time line and enjoy the great views of the Kentucky antebellum mansions across the way. A fishing pier encourages anglers of all ages to try their luck.

Sawyer Point and the riverfront are also the location of the popular **Riverfest,** held each year on September 3. The region's largest Labor Day celebration is the site of its famous fireworks and other family events, including the annual **Rubber Duck Regatta.**

Each year during Riverfest up to 40,000 rubber ducks "dive" into the Ohio River at the L&N Bridge to power paddle in heated competition toward a finish line located at the Showboat *Majestic.* Proceeds benefit a local food bank. Anyone can enter—you just have to "adopt" a duck. Past prizes have included a Toyota truck, airline tickets, a Caribbean cruise, and family computer systems. If you're not interested in adoption, watching can be just as much fun.

Also celebrated here is the **Kids Fest,** the largest free, one-day children's event in the country. With more than 100 activities—including face painting, games, and continuous entertainment—it's a sure hit each June and is sponsored by the city's Recreation Commission. The Cincinnati/ Northern Kentucky area has had a long tradition in catering to kids. In 1905 Daniel Carter Beard founded the "Sons of Daniel Boone" here, which eventually evolved into the Boy Scouts of America. For festival information call the Convention and Visitors Bureau at (800) 543–2613.

Fireworks explode over Riverfront Stadium every time the **Cincinnati Reds** thrill fans with their exciting brand of baseball. A recent survey by *Playboy* magazine named Riverfront as the least expensive of all major league parks, so you know you and your little enthusiasts will be getting a lot of exciting baseball action for your buck.

Every kid in Cincinnati grows up wanting to play baseball for the Reds. Even if you're not interested in baseball, you probably know that the team has played in nine World Series (and won five of them) and has sent 31 players to the Baseball Hall of Fame. To many locals Cincinnati and baseball go together like bacon and eggs.

It's not just that the Queen City had the first professional baseball team in the United States (it was founded in 1869). The city has been crazy about baseball since another Cincinnati resident, President William Howard Taft, threw out the first pitch in a ball game in Washington, D.C., and created a new American pastime (some would say obsession).

Baseball mania begins in April, when the Reds play their first game, and lasts through the end of the season. And Riverfront Stadium is within walking distance of most downtown hotels, making it even easier for your family to join in the spirit. Between bites of a famous ballpark hot dog (they're just $1.00) you may even find yourselves hollering "Let's Go Reds" with everyone else. For ticket information call (800) 829–5353 outside Cincinnati, 421–REDS in town.

Another view of the city skyline is available on one of the many nostalgic riverboats docked on the river. Take in a musical, comedy or dramatic revue on the **Showboat *Majestic*** (513–241–6550), the last of the original floating theaters. First launched in 1923, her builder, owner, and actor Thomas Jefferson Reynolds, raised eleven children on board while entertaining at countless river towns in the era before malls and multiscreen cinemas. Today the *Majestic* features great shows from April through October on board this National Historic Landmark.

Across the river, the riverboat ***Mike Fink*** also stays in port while offering seafood specialties and a great view of the city skyline, including the Roebling bridge, an 1867 suspension model designed by John A. Roebling that served as the prototype for the more famous Brooklyn Bridge.

While the *Majestic* and the *Mike Fink* stay docked, **BB Riverboats** still take to the languid waters of the Ohio. Located at Covington Landing across from Riverfront Stadium, the BB fleet is the city's oldest and largest and offers year-round sightseeing and dining cruises. Enjoy an all-day mini-vacation cruise, a holiday cruise, or one of the foot-stamping, toe-tapping music, entertainment, and theme cruises. There's even a "Skyline Chili Cruise" which features the best of Cincinnati's two famous "skylines"— the real one and the chili. Boats range in size from the modern 580-seat *FunLiner,* the authentic 110-seat stern-wheeler, the *Mark Twain,* and the beautiful, steamboat-era *Becky Thatcher.* For prices, reservations, and more information call (606) 261–8500.

Every three years the city is the proud host of the **Tall Stacks Festival,** which brings hundreds of boats to the riverfront for a celebration of the American steamboating era. If you're not lucky enough to visit during that time (the next one is in 1998), would-be Tom Sawyers can re-create the magic of steamboatin' with one of the many trips offered by the **Delta Queen Steamship Company.**

The first paddle wheel churned up the Ohio River in 1811 and forever changed the course of American history. Steamboating vacations, steeped in adventure, romance, and history are a legacy of nineteenth-century America and a reminder of a more gracious era.

The Queen City is one of the many colorful ports visited by the *Mississippi Queen,* the *Delta Queen,* and the new *American Queen,* launched in 1995. These overnight paddle-wheel steamboats are the last to ply our nation's rivers. America's inland rivers, an area known as "Mark Twain's America," is the setting for three- to sixteen-night cruises.

On board the sounds of a calliope—a mighty steam and iron piano— fill the area as the ship gets under way. Inside guests feast on regional specialties, including Mississippi mud pie, better known as "heaven on a plate." Afterward the rhythms of a ragtime piano and a strumming banjo (along with a few impromptu sing-alongs) keep the atmosphere lively.

The next day you can choose to explore a friendly port en route or simply relax on board. Kids enjoy tours of the ship's engine room and the pilot-house or a chance to try out the fancy calliope. For added fun, join the ships during one of their theme cruises, which include everything from all-American baseball and Civil War cruises to old-fashioned country Christmas cruises.

Itineraries include "The American South," "Crossroads of America," "America's Heartland," and "Wilderness Rivers." Cincinnati is one of the departure points, with four-, five-, and seven-night cruises available. Staterooms range from cozy inside cabins to spacious suites; all are decorated with homey prints and antique reproductions. Prices range from $490 per person for three nights to $9,420 for sixteen nights. Fares include accommodations, all meals, entertainment, daily activities, and more. For a brochure and more information call (800) 543–1949.

If you still haven't had enough water, you may want to catch a wave at **Surf Cincinnati Waterpark,** off I–275 just 5 miles west of I–75. Family entertainment and an area known as "Fun City," with a wave pool, water slides, inner-tube rapids, a lazy river to float along, and two children's rides make this a longtime local favorite. There's also concessions, volleyball, minigolf, go-carts, and always-popular bumper boats. For current ticket prices and more information call (513) 742–0620.

Think **Coney Island** is in New York? Think again. Cincy is home to this wet-and-wild entertainment complex, located just minutes from downtown at I–275 and Kellogg Avenue. Here you'll find Sunlite, the world's largest recirculating pool, the ZIPP! watercoaster, water slides, minigolf, sand volleyball, basketball, bumper boats, pedal boats, skid cars, tilt-a-whirl, Ferris wheel, kiddie rides, and more than 16 classic and family-style rides. Lifeguards even patrol in rubber rafts. Hours are 10:00 A.M. to 8:00 P.M. Memorial Day through Labor Day. Coney Island is at 6201 Kellogg Avenue. For current admission prices or more information call (513) 232–8230.

Peacocks have been known to meet and greet guests at the main entrance to the **Cincinnati Zoo and Botanical Garden.** From I–75 follow the paw prints north of downtown to "The Sexiest Zoo In America." The park was so dubbed by *Newsweek* magazine because of its successful endangered species reproduction program. Only the zoo in San Diego has a higher success rate in endangered species breeding.

Here you can check out a population of more than 750 animals. Maybe you'll catch a walrus sleeping on a rock—they turn pink in the sun—or a rare Komodo dragon emerging from its cave (these giant lizards grow to be 10 feet long and weight more than 300 pounds!). The zoo's collection of wild cats is said to be the world's most comprehensive, with nineteen different species represented.

Come prepared to spend a leisurely day wandering through one of the top five zoological parks in the nation and one of the most visited public gardens in the United States. Along the way you'll discover rare wild animals and an extensive and colorful variety of plant life.

Early morning visitors to Gibbon Island are treated to the animal's expressive calls and chatters. One the other side of the park, Wildlife Canyon boasts some of the rarest animals in the zoo's collection, including the delicate Mhorr gazelles, now extinct in the wild; the shy, diminutive zebra duikers; the rare and elusive takin; and the highly endangered Sumatran rhinoceros. A $7.5 million exhibit, Jungle Trails, features two acres of hillside and valley terrain that have been transformed into a lush, Asian–African forest for bonobos (pygmy chimps), orangutans, and smaller primates.

Gorilla World—the lush, tropical home of a lowland gorilla family led by a magnificent silverback male—is home to these gentle giants of the primate kingdom. Other not-to-miss zoo inhabitants include the lovable red pandas, the playful polar bears, and the colorful creatures who flit about in the Butterfly Aviary. Children are encouraged to pet some animals in the Spaulding Children's Zoo as well as take a peek at the adorable animal babies in the zoo's usually crowded nursery. (Zoo babies are also shown off in a festival each spring and a zoo babies' month in June.) The zoo is even fun in the winter, when more than 200 miles of lights cover the grounds and a Victorian village is centered by an ice skating rink made of 43,000 pounds of ice.

In 1992 the zoo opened part of its research facility to the public. The $4 million Carl H. Lindner, Jr. Family Center for Reproduction of Endangered Wildlife (affectionately known as "CREW") is a modern Noah's ark with fascinating "Frozen Zoo" and "Frozen Garden" exhibits. CREW researchers are credited with helping preserve wildlife for generations to come through arrested reproduction techniques. Accomplish-ments include the world's first successful birth of an exotic animal from a frozen embryo and the first successful interspecies transfer, which resulted in a surrogate eland giving birth to a bonobo.

After a full day rest your feet while your kids take a camel ride or enjoy a snack in the Safari restaurant. The zoo is open 365 days a year. Hours are 9:00 A.M. to 8:00 P.M. daily (entrance closes at 6:00 P.M.) in summer; 9:00 A.M. to 7:00 P.M. year-round (entrance closes at 5:00 P.M.). The zoo is at 3400 Vine Street; for additional information call (513) 281–4700.

JEFFERSONVILLE

Another kind of zoo can be found not far from Cincinnati. Outlet shopping has became an American obsession, with many people sharing their savvy secret with friends. On weekends and at Christmas this place can start to look like Grand Central Station.

If your family has been bitten by the bug, a good place to bag great bargains is the centrally located **Ohio Factory Shops,** which is about thirty-five minutes from Dayton, thirty-five minutes from Columbus, and fifty minutes from Cincinnati. The intersection of I–71 and U.S. 35 is the location of the state's largest outlet mall, where you'll find a parking lot full of cars and stores full of bargains.

You'll save 25–70 percent off retail prices at stores that range from Laura Ashley for adorable, old-fashioned little girl's clothes and English-style housewares to Baby Guess/Guess Kids for up-to-date school fashions. Big boys can indulge at Brooks Brothers; you can stock up on towels and sheets at the Springmaid/Wamsutta store, or pick up something for the backyard at The Nature Company, which also has great kids' toys with a geological or natural bent. More toys at bargain prices can be found at the Toy Warehouse.

None of those appeal to you? There are more than seventy-five stores in a covered, village-like setting, as well as an outdoor playground for when the kids (or you) want to blow off a little steam. The mall is open Monday through Saturday from 10:00 A.M. to 9:00 P.M., and Sunday from noon to 6:00 P.M. For directions or more information call (800) 746–7644.

SOUTHEAST OHIO

I f you think all of Ohio is flat farmland, think again. The state's many natural wonders can be found in its southeastern region, also known as "Ohio's Outback," where the land is rich with lush forests, splendid waterfalls, and rugged terrain. There are man-made wonders too: prehistoric earthworks, traditional stern-wheelers, picturesque towns, and friendly college campuses that rank among the state's oldest.

Some consider this the most undiscovered part of the state. There are no large cities. Instead you'll find sleepy, small towns with restored historic districts; country landscapes perfect for family adventures such as hiking, backpacking, or horseback riding; and quiet back roads where you can relax and discover an Ohio unknown to fast-track city residents.

CAMBRIDGE

Many of the animals that once roamed Ohio's terrain have long since vanished. It's a fact: Three animal species per day are lost to extinction. And that number is growing rapidly. It's hard to believe that prior to the twentieth century that number was only one species per year. At the current rate we could lose 20 percent of all species on earth in the next two decades. It's a sobering thought.

Help your family learn to respect the earth's varied inhabitants with a visit to **The Wilds.** This expansive preserve, situated on 9,154 acres with rolling grassland, dense forest, and cooling lakes in the northern cor-

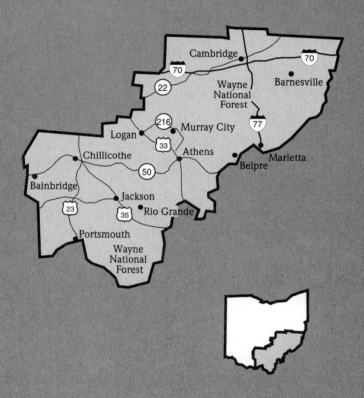

Cambridge

Wayne
National
Forest

Barnesville

70

70

22

216 Murray City

Logan

33

Athens

77

Chillicothe

Marietta

50

Belpre

Bainbridge

Jackson

23

35 Rio Grande

Portsmouth

Wayne
National
Forest

Southeast Ohio

ner of Southeast Ohio, uses state-of-the-art techniques to reproduce and protect many species of vanishing animals. The multimillion dollar effort, nearly twenty years in the works, hopes to help the animals reproduce and survive, with the goal of someday releasing some of the young into their native habitats. With 14 square miles of natural, open-range habitat, it's the first preserve of its kind in the world.

Although the preserve has a lofty mission, one of its goals is to make these animals accessible to families who will learn about them by visiting. The two relatively tame African white rhinoceroses in the pen may look ominous, but they're better known as Luanne and Momma, two rhinos who were moved here a few years ago from the Columbus Zoo.

Luanne and Momma are just two examples of the endangered species found in this peaceable kingdom. Roaming among the many acres are many animals virtually unknown to today's population, including the Przewalski wild horse from Asia; Hartmann's mountain zebra, of which fewer than 6,000 still survive in southern Africa; the North American red wolf, nearly extinct in the American Southwest; the Scimitar-horned oryx; Africa's Cuvier's gazelle, with just 400 in the wild; the Bactrian camel; Jackson's hartebeest; sable and eland antelopes; the reticulated giraffe; and trumpeter and tundra swans. Many of the animals have been given to the facility by zoos that support the preserve's mission and want to see animals in danger of extinction survive.

Visitors see many of these species on the forty-five-minute shuttle tour of the grounds. Few of the animals seem bothered by the buses—some, including a shaggy female Bactrian camel, refuse to move from the road when buses want to get by. A few seem just as curious about their human visitors, craning their necks as the buses roll by.

The Wilds is a new facility and as such is just getting set up. There's currently a visitors center, a bookstore, a snack shop, and some picnic sites. Future plans include a lodge and the development of safari wilderness camps.

The Wilds is at 14000 International Road, off State Route 340. Tours are $6.00 for adults, $4.00 for children. For more information call (614) 638–5030.

MURRAY CITY

Does a Western-style family adventure exist in Southeast Ohio? You betcha, pardner. Cowpokes, rustlers, and just regular folks saddle up for getaways at the **Smoke Rise Ranch Resort,** a working cattle ranch not far from cosmopolitan Athens that offers guests the opportunity to experience Western adventures closer to home. If you saw *City Slickers* and want a taste of that life, this is the vacation for you.

Experience the famed cowboy lifestyle as you and your kids participate in cattle drives, team penning, cow cutting, and guided trail rides. Or if you prefer just relax on the more than 2,000 acres of scenic, privately owned land. Located just 7 miles from Burr Oak State Park and bordered by a wildlife management area and the Wayne National Forest, the ranch has places to fish, abundant wildlife, more than 100 miles of well-groomed trails for riding, and more.

The ranch is owned and operated by the Semingson family, who have been in the ranching business all of their lives. As apprentice ranch hands, your family will spend time in the saddle rounding up strays, doctoring sick calves, checking fences, and driving the herd. Guests stay in rustic, bunk-style cabins that sleep up to six people and cook in their cabins or eat in the main dining area. But it's not too rustic; there's also a heated swimming pool and playground, hot tub, and a clubhouse with a kitchen. Activities include pool parties, barbecues, music, and dancing. Smoke Rise also offers a diverse outdoor-education program with a certified naturalist at The Outpost, which has hour-long hikes to weeklong experiences. Parents can enroll their school-age children and free time for themselves to ride, take lessons, or just relax.

Family weeklong vacations include six nights' cabin accommodations, six days' horse rental, riding lessons, full use of facilities, and other options. Prices range from $480 without meals for one person to $2,415 for a family of six with meals. Weekend vacations with two nights' accommodations are also available, as are overnight stays and camping hookups. For more information contact the resort at 82 North Court Street, Athens, 45701 (800–292–1732).

KHRISTI'S TOP FAMILY ADVENTURES IN SOUTHEAST OHIO

1. Ohio River Museum, Marietta
2. The Wilds, Cambridge
3. Lee Middleton Original Doll Factory, Belpre
4. Hocking Hills, Logan
5. Bob Evans Farm, Rio Grande

LOGAN

Some consider the **Hocking Hills** the state's crown jewels—as well as some of the most un-Ohio-like terrain in Ohio. They're spectacular year-round, with caves, rugged gorges and wooded cliffs, and views that go on for miles, but they're especially breathtaking in the fall, when leaves on the many trees turn varying shades of russet, gold, and scarlet. Located about 15 miles west of Logan, the hills offer a panorama of Ohio geology. Park naturalists like to brag that the Hocking Hills area is a cross between Canada in the valleys and Carolina and Tennessee in the ridges.

The hills are full of superlatives. Here you'll find the state's *largest* natural rock bridge, its *deepest* gorge, *highest* waterfall, and *largest* recessed cave, all in one area. The scenic valleys and Appalachian foothills in this southeastern Ohio county create a recreational haven where hikers, canoeists, rock climbers, rappelers, equestrians, backpackers, fishermen, bicyclists, hunters, birders, or families just out for a breath of fresh air will find a welcome retreat.

Your family will find exciting activities in 2,000-acre **Hocking Hills State Park** year-round, including sparkling waterfalls and rock formations laden with lore and legend. Follow the trails to Ash Cave, where a 90-foot waterfall marks the spot where Indians once camped, and to Old Man's Cave, a former Civil War hermit's haunt and the site of three more stunning cascades and the intriguing rock formation known as the Devil's Bathtub. Junior shutterbugs and family-vacation chroniclers shouldn't miss a shot of the scenic cliffs at Cedar Falls, voted the most photogenic waterfall in the state (you'll also find the state's tallest tree, a 149-foot hemlock), or the observation platform along Rim Trail, with an unsurpassed view of the deep gorge and rare plants that thrive in the strangely named Conkles Hollow (no one knows who Conkle was, but he left his mark on the gorge: W. J. CONKLE 1797). Another must-see: Cantwell Cliffs, with breathtaking 150-foot-high walls (better be in shape: there are hundreds of steps), and the age-old Rock House (where water has slowly carved "rooms" in the side of a cliff), which has a colorful history as a robber's roost (it's also a favorite picnic spot). Rock House was such a popular tourist attraction in the early 1800s that a sixteen-room hotel, complete with ballroom and a U.S. Post Office, was built nearby.

Hoping for more comfortable rooms for an overnight stay? The state park also rents out forty comfortable cabins with two bedrooms, bath with shower, fully equipped kitchen with microwave, linens, and a gas fireplace ($68–$84) or you can opt to sleep under the stars in the campgrounds. Cabins are reserved by the week in summer; fall weekends should be reserved a year in advance. The park is off State Route 664 about 15 miles southeast of Logan. For more information call (614) 385–6841. For more information on the Hocking Hills area call (800) HOCKING.

Ever wanted to sleep in a log cabin? You can pretend you're a pioneer family during a stay in an original 1800s-era hand-hewn log cabin, restored with a fully equipped kitchen and bath (all you bring are toiletries and food). Located on Hocking County's Skyline Drive, each of the **Frontier Log Cabins** has a fireplace and was constructed of hand-hewn logs from the nearby Hocking Forest. Cabins are located in a secluded area of a forty-year-old white pine forest in Laurelville and are available year-round. For more information contact 18381 Thompson Ridge Road, Laurelville 43135 or call (614) 332–6747.

Laurelville is also the home of the only known company in Ohio

TOP ANNUAL EVENTS IN SOUTHEAST OHIO

River Recreation Festival, July, Gallipolis; (800) 765–6482

Kidfest!, Athens; (614) 593–3988

Bob Evans Farm Festival, October, Rio Grande; (800) 288–FARM

Ohio River Sternwheel Festival, September, Marietta; (800) 288–2577

founded by children—the **On Our Own General Country Store.** Take your would-be entrepreneurs here for a lesson or two from three sisters—now ages sixteen, eighteen, and nineteen—who figure their own books and keep shop the old-fashioned way: without the aid of a clock, calculator, or cash register. The girls jointly conceived of a business when they were ages seven, nine, and eleven and talked their parents into a cider slush stand at the family's adjacent Laurelville Fruit Company. With a little help from their friends and family, the girls built the log store, did the caulking, stripping, and staining themselves, and filled it with edible goodies and country-style decorating supplies. Your kids may never be content with a simple lemonade stand again. The country store is at 16197 Pike Street and is open seasonally. Mom runs it while they're in school. For more information call (614) 332–2621.

All aboard! Another popular attraction in the area is the **Hocking Valley Scenic Railway** in historic Nelsonville, about thirty minutes away from the Hocking Hills State Park. Engine No. 33, an oldtime passenger train, offers railway enthusiasts a leisurely ride back in time through the beautiful hills of southeastern Ohio.

Relive the romance of the rails as the historic locomotives and passenger coaches carry you over century-old tracks through the Wayne National Forest and a right of way listed on the National Register of Historic Sites, passing brick kilns and a canal lock along the way. Enjoy the blooming dogwood trees in the spring, the lush acreage in the summer, and the spectacular fall foliage in autumn. There's even a special winter ride with holiday poems, stories, music, and old St. Nick on the "Santa Train," a perennial favorite with tiny train buffs (early reservations are recommended).

The train transports visitors through areas not visible from roadways. Trains also stop at **Robbins Crossing,** an 1860s settler village at Hocking College. There are two departures daily from the railway depot at U.S. Route 33 and Hocking Parkway Drive on weekends from Memorial Day through October. Routes include a 12-mile trip to Haydenville at noon and a 25-mile trip to Logan at 2:30 P.M. For more information contact the railroad at P.O. Box 427, Nelsonville, 45764 (614–753–9531).

CHILLICOTHE

Take Route 23 south from Columbus and you'll run directly into Chillicothe, once the capital of Ohio. It's one of the oldest towns in the state, with impressive Victorian-era buildings and long rows of peaceful residential streets. It's a great place to enjoy a relaxing day wandering through the many shops and soaking up the city's long and varied history.

While the town will celebrate its bicentennial in 1996, its history actually began in *pre*history, when the area was the home of the mound-building Hopewell and Adena Indians, a culture known as the "Egyptians of the United States" because of the amount of building they did. At one time the Hopewell culture stretched across the United States; many of their burial and ceremonial mounds, however, are found in Southern Ohio.

The **Hopewell Culture National Historic Park** preserves twenty-three remaining ceremonial mounds and runs an innovative "Junior Ranger" program for kids that teaches them about the park and the long-ago people who built it.

A free Junior Ranger booklet guides families through the highlights of the park, including an on-site museum and visitors center. While in the visitors center, don't miss the award-winning "Legacy of the Moundbuilders," a fifteen-minute video that recounts the lives and lore of the Hopewell. There's also a well-stocked bookstore with books on archaeology and Indian culture for adults and children.

After visiting, kids are encouraged to fill out the questionnaire in the

Junior Ranger booklet; they're then "sworn in" as honorary Junior Rangers, complete with badge. The park is open year-round from 8:30 A.M. to 5:00 P.M. It's located at 16062 State Route 104. For more information call (614) 774-1125.

Southeast Ohio's earliest days are also the subject of **Tecumseh!,** a spectacular reenactment of the life and times of the great Shawnee leader. A large tiered amphitheater nestled in the hardwood forest of Sugarloaf Mountain has become a mecca for more than a million annual tourists from all over the world who come to sit among birds and forest and be carried back through time to another world.

The show has garnered accolades from around the country: "Easily the most massive and impressive outdoor spectacle east of the Mississippi," says the *Richmond Times Dispatch;* "It ought to be required viewing for every schoolchild in Ohio," claims the *Troy Daily News.*

Here, under the stars, kids watch wide-eyed as horses gallop down from the hills, arrows wing overhead, and artillery thunders through the surrounding country. At any time, crossfire threatens half the audience. While the performance has been occasionally criticized for taking "literary license" with history, it's a sure way to get your children interested in the lives of men and women who lived and died long ago.

Another sure hit with families is the backstage tour, offered every hour from 2:00 to 5:00 P.M. Monday through Saturday. Cast members serve as guides, providing a historical background of the area and theater before leading visitors backstage through the lighting, set, props, techniques, and pyrotechnics. As part of the tour, the stuntmen give lively displays of stage combat and flintlock firing, and even pitch headfirst from a 21-foot cliff. Afterward they get up and explain how they did it to a fascinated, adoring crowd. Tours are just $3.50 for adults, $2.00 for children age ten and younger.

There's also a free prehistoric Indian minimuseum, with artifacts from the first settlers of Ohio Country; a restaurant overlooking a vista of forests and mountains, featuring a popular buffet from 4:30 to 7:45 P.M. each evening ($7.00 for adults, $3.75 for children age ten and younger); and the Mountain Valley gift shop, across from the box office, with handcrafted Indian jewelry, pottery, and other gifts and souvenirs.

Tickets for *Tecumseh!* are $11 to $13 for adults, $6.00 for children age ten and younger. For tickets and reservations call (614) 775–0700.

While in Chillicothe, check out the tiny, authentic 1930s diner known as **Carl's Townhouse,** whose motto is "A Clean Place to Eat." This neighborhood joint is where families come in for the justly famous single, double, or triple hamburgers and homemade soups such as bean and vegetable, and where regulars still tally up their own bill. John Goodwill has owned Carl's since 1951; he recently added **Goody's Goodies** next door, a classic ice cream parlor. Carl's is at 95 South Paint Street (614–773–1660).

Not far away is the **Bavarian Toy Works,** where kids (and kids at heart) will be tempted to spend their next year's allowance in advance. Jim Lungo, a toy connoisseur who was always given quality toys by his aunts, runs the shop. Parts of the building date back to before Ohio became a state. The brick-floored basement houses an educational center and games; upstairs, regimental soldiers and puppets are displayed in a cabinet across from an old cherry fireplace mantel. There are more than twenty different lines of dolls, including some that can be played with. There's also a nice selection of children's books and collectible bears, including Steiff and Hermann. The store is at 31 South Paint Street. For information call (614) 775–4502.

BAINBRIDGE

Bring the hiking boots when you head out for a visit to the **Seven Caves.** West of Bainbridge off U.S. Route 50, spelunkers' fantasies come true. Lace up and follow the three nature trails into the caves, where you'll find cement walks, handrails, and push-button lighting that emphasizes formations along the way. Cliffs, canyons, waterfalls, and more than 300 species of plants and trees are found in the adjacent park. The caves are open year-round and located at 7660 Cave Road. Admission is $7.00 for adults; $3.50 for children age five to eleven. Hours are 8:00 A.M. to dark daily. For more information call (513) 365–1283.

PORTSMOUTH

This Ohio River town is the gateway to the **Shawnee State Forest,** also known as Ohio's "Little Smokies." Nestled in the Appalachian foothills on the banks of the Ohio River, the state park and the state forest is a dramatically hilly wilderness area of nearly 62,000 acres of unbroken land. It's the largest contiguous forest in the state, with so many trees that a constant blue haze seems to hang in the air, giving the park an ethereal, other-worldly feeling.

Partaking of worldly pleasures such as horseback riding and back-packing is the best way to see the park. In spring the hillsides are splashed with wildflowers; in fall a spectacular spray of colors brightens the vista. You can also drive your car along the 170 miles of roadway that are main-tained by the Division of Forestry. If you do nothing else, don't miss the Panoramic Scenic Loop Drive for its route through the forest and its unfor-gettable overlooks.

Although camping is available at the park's deluxe facility (there are 107 sites), many guests opt to stay in the fifty-room **Shawnee Resort and Conference Center,** opened in 1973. While stocked with modern con-veniences, the lodge has a rustic, Native American flavor that families find irresistible. Big stone fireplaces, timber framing, arrow and spear collec-tions, and a full-size birchbark canoe add to the ambience. Guest rooms sport furnishings crafted by local artisans.

The lodge's outdoor pool and sundeck have a great view of Turkey Foot Lake and the park's ragged ridges. There are also an indoor pool, whirlpool, sauna, and exercise room. Rooms—many with vaulted ceilings and pine walls—are spacious and feature Native American designs and nature posters. The lodge also has twenty-five family cabins on a ridge near the lodge. There's also an eighteen-hole championship golf course adjacent to the Ohio River, fishing, boating, tennis, game room, and hayrides.

To get to the lodge take State Route 52 west of Portsmouth to Route 125. Rates change seasonally. Shawnee is part of the **Ohio State Park Resorts and Conference Centers,** which operate eight great family-style resorts throughout the state. For information, current rates, and reserva-tions call (800) 282–7275.

WAYNE NATIONAL FOREST

Encompassing an area of more than 200,000 acres spread out across sev-eral southeastern counties, the vast **Wayne National Forest** is the state's only national forest. There are plenty of free opportunities for camping, hiking, picnicking, fishing, horseback riding, and even specially marked trails for off-road vehicles, something not found in other area parks.

Like ghost towns? Along the hiking trails here are remnants of abandoned cabin and homestead sites and other eerie signs of former inhabitants. You'll also pass the remains of a one-room schoolhouse, an oil well, and an abandoned farmhouse. Year-round you'll find evidence of the abundant wildlife and plant life that characterize this beautiful and rugged land. And if you'd like to pitch a tent and sleep under the stars, no permits are necessary, although state licenses are necessary for hunting, fishing, and gathering firewood.

For information or maps on activities within the Wayne National Forest write 219 Columbus Road, Athens, 45701 or call (614) 592–6644.

RIO GRANDE

Your family has eaten the sausage a hundred times, but did you know that Bob Evans was a real person? And that he really did live "down on the farm"?

The **Bob Evans Farm** in Rio Grande, not far from the West Virginia border, was home to Bob Evans, founder of the Bob Evans Farms, for nearly twenty years. Bob and his wife Jewel raised their six children in the large brick farmhouse known as the Homestead. A former stagecoach stop and inn, the house is now listed on the National Register of Historic Places.

It was here that Bob first made the sausage that would make him famous. In 1946 he whipped up a batch for the twelve-stool, twenty-four-hour restaurant he had opened in nearby Gallipolis, Ohio. As a sideline, he sold ten-pound tubs of sausage to restaurant patrons, eventually expanding his distribution to nearby grocery stores. As his popularity grew, Bob invited clients to come "down on the farm" to see where the sausage was made.

As more and more people came, however, he decided to open a little sausage shop. The Sausage Shop, which is now a Bob Evans Restaurant, was the company's first venture into the restaurant business.

After a hearty breakfast at the restaurant (the biscuits are second to none), grab a paddle and head for Raccoon Creek (really a river, but the old name stuck), where the waters are blue-green and make for adventurous canoeing. Or saddle up for a spin around the farm via horseback. Want to stay on *terra firma?* The barnyard has a passel of friendly farm animals that love to be petted.

Visit Bob Evans Farm and introduce the family to a passel of friendly farm animals that love to be petted. (Courtesy Bob Evans Farm)

While there take a hike among the farm's 1,100 acres of rolling hills or peruse the museum of farm implements and farm life. An authentic log cabin provides insights into a bygone way of life. And if you're here in October, don't miss the annual Bob Evans Farm Festival, with more than 100 craftspeople, country entertainment (including an apple-peeling, corn-shelling, a feed-sack race, a cow-chip throwing contest, and hog-calling) as well as tractor pulls, wagon rides and—of course—plenty of food.

The Bob Evans Farm is at State Route 588 just off State Route 35 in Rio Grande. Hours are 8:30 A.M. to 5:00 P.M. daily from Memorial Day weekend through Labor Day as well as weekends in September. For more information call (800) 994–FARM.

MARIETTA

Westward, ho! In many ways, the U.S. westward expansion began with the establishment of the city of Marietta.

This southern Ohio city was the first organized American settlement in the U.S.'s Northwest Territory and the state's "first" city. The original forty-seven pioneers of the Ohio Company arrived in Marietta from New England by flatboat in 1788. Many of the settlers were veteran officers of the Revolutionary War who received land in lieu of cash for their wartime services. Farsighted and community minded, they designed wide streets lined with beautiful homes as well as parks and common areas. In honor of Queen Marie Antoinette of France they named the city "Marietta."

Luckily, the city has enjoyed a better fate than its namesake. Today many of those historic sites remain and many more attractions have been added, making Marietta one of the state's most charming and fascinating destinations. In many ways it appears as if a little bit of New England has been transplanted to the Ohio prairie.

For an up-close view of the city, consider a ride in a vintage horse-drawn carriage. **Classic Carriage** takes families back in time as they clip-clop down brick-lined streets through the historic city. Rides depart from the front of the Lafayette Hotel on Friday and Saturday nights and are $10 per person. For more information call (614) 667–3513.

Although not quite as old a means of transportation, the city's **Trolley Tours** are loads of fun. Hop on board one of these beauties and, with the clang-clang of the bell, you're off on a tour that takes in all the city's highlights, including the Victorian-style shops along Front Street, Marietta College, and more. Trips are offered April to October and cost $7.50 per adult, $5.00 per child. For schedules and more information call (614) 374–2233.

Today the **Campus Martius Museum** sits on the site of the city's original fortification. Newly restored, it preserves the history of Marietta, early Ohio, and the Northwest Territory. With original pioneer artifacts, original maps, tools, furnishings, agricultural implements, and even a full-size home, it preserves a way of life long since past in the state. If your kids have only seen covered Conestoga wagons in TV westerns, here's your chance to show them the real thing.

The full-size home once belonged to Rufus Putnam, superintendent of the Ohio Company of Associates, the landholders responsible for Marietta's settlement. You can't help but wander through the rooms of the simple, plank structure and wonder at the hard lives of the people who once lived here or what the walls have seen and heard. The oldest home in the state, the house still stands in its original location and is the only surviving dwelling of the original fortification.

The land office of the Ohio Company, from which portions of the land were divvied up, is also housed here. The museum is at 601 Second Street and is open 9:30 A.M. to 5:00 P.M. weekdays, noon to 5:00 P.M. weekends most of the year. For more information call (614) 373–3750.

History of another kind is found at the city's charming **Children's Toy and Doll Museum** on Maple Street. Located in a restored B&O passenger train car in historic Harmar Village, it's a family favorite and a surefire hit with younger children. Three of the most enchanting highlights include the talking dollhouse, which tells the story of a Christmas wedding circa 1900; the Cook Dollhouse, which contains miniatures from all over the world; and the Betsy Ross Dollhouse, built the day after she made America's first flag. Can't wait till Christmas? Get ready for Santa with a trip to his workshop, where tiny elves work around the clock to get ready for that special day.

Also found here are Marietta's first teddy bear, baby dolls, games and collections, and a host of other old beloved toys. The museum is open from 1:00 to 5:00 P.M. daily (except Monday) from June through September. Admission is $1.00; children under age 6 are free. For more information call (614) 373–5900.

You know it's the real thing, but did you know that there's a whole museum devoted to Coca-Cola? In the three years since **Butch's Cola Museum** has been in existence, it has attracted collectors and the curious from all fifty states as well as sixty-six foreign countries. The museum chronicles the rise (and rise and rise) of this beloved soft drink. Butch started ed collecting Coke memorabilia some seventeen years ago. As his collection took off he moved it to the museum, where it now spotlights memorabilia from 1900 to the present. The collection includes signs, coolers, machines, and paper items that he's accumulated over the years, including a rare 1900 Icy-O cooler, one of only six remaining in the world. There's also a gift shop and a model of an old country store. The museum is at 118 Maple Street. Hours vary with the season. Admission is 50 cents per adult; kids are admitted free or just $1.00 for the entire family. For more information call (614) 376–COKE.

Steamboatin' plays a large part in the city's history and psyche. One of the city's liveliest events is the **Ohio River Sternwheel Festival,** held for three days each September. Marietta is home of the American Sternwheel Association and the rightful host of this annual event.

Included in the festivities is entertainment from calliope to jazz, the crowning of the "Queen Genevieve Of The River" during a headliner concert, and a dazzling fireworks display. Sunday brings riverside church services and the grand finale: the colorful, hard-fought sternwheel races. For dates and more information call (614) 373–5178.

For a lively account of the sternwheel's history, check out the **Ohio River Museum** on Front Street. It chronicles the exciting era in which elegant steamboats and floating hotels plied the Ohio.

After the Civil War, however, railroads cut into the steamboats' profits. Quicker speeds, better cargo handling, and easier scheduling enticed travelers and businesses to switch allegiance to the new mode of transportation. Soon, the less efficient steamboats were all but retired from the river.

Today, remnants of that proud past can be found preserved in museums. The one in Marietta, opened in 1974, is one of the best and most comprehensive. A good first stop is the full-sized diorama that re-creates the wildlife found along an Ohio waterway two centuries ago. A thirty-minute video on steamboat history entitled "Fire On The Water" explores the often-dangerous days when boilers were known to explode, killing hundreds, and contains footage of both old excursion boats and present-day steamboats such as the *Delta Queen* (rest assured: most of today's steamboats are diesel-powered and driven by propellers while a fake sternwheel is moved by the passing water).

Here you'll also find one of the oldest existing steamboat pilothouses, from the *Tell City,* built in 1885. Kids will get a kick out of standing behind the wooden wheel and pretending they're the captain, piloting the boat down the river. Along with scaled-down riverboat models, ornate cabin furnishings, and other memorabilia from the golden age of steamboat travel, the museum offers a full-size example, the *W. P. Snyder,* the sole surviving steam-powered sternwheel towboat in the United States. Another crowd-pleaser is the school of carp that takes up summer residence beside the towboat *W. P. Snyder, Jr.,* in order to feed on the bread

that visitors throw. The carp—like the swallows at San Juan Capistrano—
are so faithful to the locale that they return each April.

The museum is located at Front and St. Clair streets; hours vary with
the season. Admission is $4.00 for adults, $1.00 for children age six to twelve;
children under age six free. For more information call (614) 373-3750.

If you'd love to ride one of these beauties, a number of local compa-
nies offer riverboat excursions along the Ohio and Muskingum Rivers.
From May through November, your family can enjoy a ride on the *Valley
Gem Sternwheeler,* a Coast Guard approved authentic sternwheeler built
in 1988. With its big paddle wheel churning up the river, it's a slice of
Americana you won't find anywhere else. George Bush even dropped by
once for a ride during a presidential campaign visit. It docks at the
Washington Street Landing, adjacent to the Ohio River Museum.

Most passengers on the 300-seat boat opt for the hour-long narrated
tours at $4.50 for adults; $3.00 for children age two to twelve. Dinner
cruises are also offered on Saturday evenings with a buffet meal. Special
fall-foliage tours on weekends in October ply the scenic river on three- to
four-hour excursions ($13.00 for adults, $6.00 for kids). For times and
more information call (614) 373-7862.

Another vintage sternwheeler, the *Becky Thatcher,* attracts hundreds
of passengers but never leaves port. With parts built in the 1890s and the
1920s, she once plied the Mississippi and Ohio Rivers and hosted three
presidents during a stint as an Army Corps boat used for visiting dignitaries.
She ended up in Marietta after being towed thousands of miles for the
city's bicentennial celebration and never left.

Today she's known as the **Showboat *Becky Thatcher.*** The old boil-
er room has become a theater where talent from all over the country enter-
tains crowds in lively melodramas such as *Little Mary Sunshine* and one-
man plays including *Ring, Ring the Banjo: An Evening With Stephen
Foster* (Foster, for the uninitiated, was the composer of such classics as "Oh
Susanna," "Camptown Races," and "My Old Kentucky Home"). Villains,
heroes, and heroines are introduced to the audience at the beginning of the
performance; placards even instruct you when to boo and cheer.

Afterward wet your whistle upstairs, where the upper deck houses
the Becky Thatcher restaurant, featuring an enthusiastic waitstaff serving

steak, chicken, seafood, and a dessert known as Riverboat pie, made with coffee ice cream and other secret ingredients. For theater reservations call (614) 373–6033; for restaurant information call (614) 373–4130.

BELPRE

It's only fitting that the **Lee Middleton Original Doll Factory** on Washington Boulevard in Belpre (about 13 miles south of Marietta) look like a giant dollhouse, complete with fancy gingerbread trim. Inside, big and little enthusiasts alike watch with fascination as the highly collectible and incredibly realistic dolls by sculptor Lee Middleton Urick are made right before their eyes. Urick began sculpting dolls at her kitchen table and is the first original doll artist to build and manage a major manufacturing facility to create her work.

Middleton specializes in both porcelain and vinyl dolls, many life-sized. At the factory, families can take a tour that walks them through the entire process—from molding, filling with vinyl, and baking to hand painting and body stuffing. Tours take about thirty minutes, depending on the number of questions, a guide says.

Afterward try and resist a visit to the nursery, where you can adopt a life-sized Middleton baby (they wear real zero-to-three-month-sized baby clothes!), complete with papers, promises, and pictures. All dolls are signed and numbered. The company even makes officially licensed dolls for Hershey's, including two known as "Hershey's Kisses" dressed in gold and silver lamé.

Prices for a Middleton creation can reach up to $1,790 for the newest addition—a 36-inch porcelain doll named Elise dressed as a Civil War lady, complete with seven layers of petticoats. Only 200 will be made. Collectors and children looking for something a little less expensive should check out the less-than-perfect section in the gift shop, where dolls have minor flaws undetectable to the layman, or the bargain "store editions" that are put together with leftover outfits and materials.

Tours are offered hourly from 9:00 A.M. to 3:00 P.M. Monday through Friday. Lee Middleton dolls are also found in shops throughout the state. The factory is at 1301 Washington Boulevard. For more information call (614) 423–1481.

Be sure to visit the Lee Middleton Original Doll Factory gift shop after a tour of the factory.
(Courtesy Lee Middleton Original Doll Factory)

BARNESVILLE

This peaceful town was settled by the Quakers in the early 1800s and has a well-preserved historic district. Most little girls, however, care only for the **Barbara Barbe Doll Museum,** stuffed to the rafters with hundreds of beguiling nineteenth- and twentieth-century dolls.

Five rooms in a former 1836 women's seminary make up the small museum that displays more than 800 of the 3,500 dolls collected by former Barnesville resident Barbe. When she died, her three sons were at a loss as to what to do with the collection. Today, it attracts thousands of doll collectors, crafters, and enthusiastic little girls who ooh and aah over the German, French, and American bisque dolls, the dolls from around the world (most dressed in original costumes), and the extensive Barbie Doll collection, which takes up one whole room. Admission is $2.00; children under age six free. Hours are 1:00 to 4:00 P.M. Wednesday through Sunday from May 1 through September 30; tours are by appointment year-round. The museum is at 211 North Chestnut Street (614–425–2301).

ATHENS

Home of Ohio University, Athens is a pleasing mix of Appalachia and academia tucked into the hills of southeast Ohio. The brick streets of "uptown" Athens pulsate with the energy of more than 18,000 students, with lively shops and eateries that cater to young tastes and interests. Although urbane in many senses, it's also the gateway to the coal country of West Virginia. There are places to buy both sushi and sickles.

Athens is also home to **Southeastern Ohio Cultural Arts Center,** more affectionately known as the Dairy Barn. Not surprisingly it was once part of a dairy farm, part of the Athens Asylum where patients milked cows as part of their therapy. A community arts center in the truest sense, today the spacious center attracts the *crème de la crème* of national and international folk art. It features four to five exhibitions each year. Quilt National, held every other summer, attracts thousands of entries and visitors each year. The annual children's holiday festival features hayrides, storytellers, crafts, and more. Admission $3.00 for adults, free for children under age twelve. The arts center is at 8000 Dairy Lane (614–592–4981).

JACKSON

If huge zoos and theme parks are too much for your preschoolers, **Noah's Ark Animal Farm** may be the answer. Located on Route 32 southwest of Athens, it's home to more than 150 exotic animals and birds. Now in its eleventh season, the small-scale park was the dream of a local businessman and his wife who traveled around the country with their sons. Along the way they stopped at and were inspired by small animal and theme parks in Pennsylvania and Wisconsin.

Later they combined their love of animals, railroads, farming, and golfing into the thirty-five-acre farm. Today, kids from all over the country are enchanted by the chance to view and feed the animals (North American black bears, cougars, raccoons, pygmy goats, llamas, wild turkeys, and more), ride the 3/4-mile loop on the antique miniature train, shoot a round of eighteen-hole miniature golf, or burn off some steam in the playground. You can also build up your muscles on the paddleboats ($3.00 per half hour), fish at Pay Lake, which is stocked weekly, or toss a horseshoe or two at the recreation area ($2.00 per adult, $1.50 per child).

Farm admission is $4.50 for adults; $3.50 for children age three through twelve. The recreation area is open April 1 through December 15; the farm are is open April 1 through October 30. Hours are 10:00 A.M. to 6:00 P.M. Monday through Saturday; noon to 7:00 P.M. on Sunday. Noah's Ark is at 1527 McGiffins Road, just 5 miles east of Jackson on the Appalachian Highway. For more information call (614) 384–3060 or (800) 282–2167.

GENERAL INDEX

Sun Watch Thirteenth Century Indian
    Village, 101
Surf Cincinnati Waterpark, 122

Tall Stacks Festival, 121
Tecumseh!, 133
The Beach, 104
The Golden Lamb, 105
The Wilds, 125
Thomas Edison's Birthplace, 19
Thurber House, 76
Thurn's, 72
Toft's Dairy, 19
Toledo Botanical Gardens, 7
Toledo Mud Hens, 8
Toledo Museum of Art, 4
Toledo Zoo, 6
Tony Packo's Cafe, 3
Topiary Garden, 76
Tower City Center, 35, 41
Trolley Tours, Cleveland, 30
Trolley Tours, Marietta, 138
Twins Days Festival, 44

Underground Railroad Memorial, 29
U.S. Air Force Museum, 99
U.S. Glass Specialty Outlet, 4

U.S. Plastics Corporation, 24
University Circle, 36
USS Cod, 31

Valley Gem Sternwheeler, 141
Vermilion Lighthouse, 28
Village Bakery, 63
Village Ice Cream Parlor, 107
Village Pump Restaurant, 12

Wahkeena, 91
Wayne National Forest, 135
Wendy's, 74
Western Reserve Historical Society, 39
Wexner Center for the Arts, 77
William G. Mather Museum, 31
Willis B. Boyer, 3
Wolcott House Museum Complex, 8
Wright Cycle Company and Hoover
    Block, 98
Wyandot Lake Waterpark, 84
Wyandot Popcorn Museum, 87

Yoder's Amish Home, 50

Zane Caverns, 95
Zoar Village, 60

ACTIVITIES INDEX

AMUSEMENT PARKS
Americana Amusement Park, 105
Cedar Point, 16
Coney Island, 122
Geauga Lake, 46
Paramount King's Island, 103
Sea World, 45

CAVES
Crystal Cave, 14
Ohio Caverns, 94
Olentangy Indian Caverns, 85
Perry's Cave, 13
Seven Caves, 134
Seneca Caverns, 20
Zane Caverns, 95

BOATS/CRUISES
BB Riverboats, 121
Crystal Lady, 68
Delta Queen Steamship Company, 121
Emerald Empress, 18
Goodtime I, 19
Goodtime III, 30
M.V. City of Sandusky, 18
Nautica Queen, 30
Santa Maria, 68
Showboat *Becky Thatcher,* 141
Showboat *Majestic,* 120
USS Cod (Submarine), 31
Valley Gem Sternwheeler, 141
William G. Mather Museum, 31
Willis B. Boyer, 3

NATURE CENTERS/ ANIMAL PRESERVES

PARKS/RECREATION AREAS

RAILROADS

RESTAURANTS

Tony Packo's Cafe, 3
Village Ice Cream Parlor, 107
Village Pump Restaurant, 12
Wendy's, 74

SHOPPING
A Show of Hands, 70
Bavarian Toy Works, 134
Book Loft, 72
Cincy Shop, 110
Columbus City Center Mall, 70
Glass Heritage Gallery, 22
Hausfrau Haven, 72
Mill St. Candy Co., 53
My Little Red Wagon, 53
Ohio Factory Shops, 124
On Our Own General Country Store,
    131
Quaker Square, 52
Quaker Train Shop, 53

SPORTS
Boston Mills Ski Resort, 49
Brandywine Ski Resort, 49
Cincinnati Reds, 120
Columbus Clippers, 78
Gateway Ballpark and Arena, 34
Jacobs Field, 34
Lake Erie fishing, 10
Pro Football Hall of Fame, 57
Toledo Mud Hens, 8

THEATER
Akron Civic Theater, 53
Blue Jacket Outdoor Drama, 102
Carousel Dinner Theater, 56
Cincinnati Playhouse In The Park, 113
Cleveland Playhouse, 35
Karamu House, 37
Ohio Theater, 70
Playhouse Square, 35
Robert D. Lindner Family Omnimax
    Theater, 114
Tecumseh!, 133

TOURS
Anheuser–Busch Brewery Tours, 82
Anthony–Thomas Candy Company, 82
ASM International, 65

Ballreich's Potato Chip Company, 21
Candlelight Garten Tour, 72
Classic Carriage Tour, 138
Creegan Company, 62
Haus und Garten Tour, 72
Lee Middleton Original Doll Factory, 142
Malley's Chocolates, 34
Maxwell Crystal, 21
Olympia Gourmet Chocolates, 34
Piatt Castles, West Liberty, 93
Trolley Tours, Cleveland, 30
Trolley Tours, Marietta, 138
U.S. Plastics Corporation, 24
U.S. Glass Specialty Shop, 4

WATER PARKS
Magic Waters, 57
Surf Cincinnati Waterpark, 122
Wyandot Lake Waterpark, 84

ZOOS
Akron Zoological Park, 53
Cincinnati Zoo and Botanical Garden, 122
Cleveland MetroParks Zoo, 40
Columbus Zoo, 83
Toledo Zoo, 6

OTHER
Amish Country, 49
Carew Tower Observatory, 110
Imaginarium, 70
Inventure Place, 53
James A. Rhodes State Office Tower
    Building, 70
Johnson Island, 16
Kelley's Island, 12
Lakeside, 15
Lonz Winery, 14
Marblehead Lighthouse, 15
Middle Bass Island, 14
NASA Lewis Research Center, 41
Oberlin College, 29
Ohio Capitol Square Complex, 69
Ohio State University, 77
Put-in-Bay, 13
University Circle, 36